52 Doodles in 52 Weeks

Snaring Woodland Creatures in 2009

by

Thom Phelps

.o TABLE of CONTENTS o.

For Betta, my love.
You are the bacon on my BLT of life.

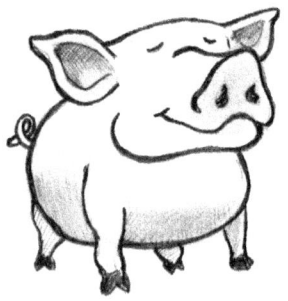

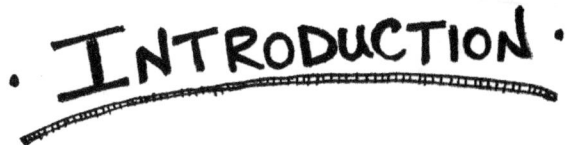

· INTRODUCTION ·

As the 2009 New Year approached, I resolved to do something creative, bright and cheerful that I could share with my friends. The previous two years had been pretty rough for everybody, and I wanted to turn over a new, optimistic leaf.

I doodle two or three times a week when I'm taking notes in meetings, so I decided to refocus the energy that I was already spending on that and train it on my creative goal. All I needed to do was lay down a few guidelines.

I promised myself one doodle or sketch of an animal per week, posted on the web in a blog (journal). Then I added a few extra conditions, like "happy," "family-friendly," and "no politics" for good measure. I called the blog "Snaring Woodland Creatures" in that I was capturing them doing not-so-everyday activities.

52 doodles in 52 weeks

It doesn't seem very ambitious when I phrase it like that. One doodle per week? Piece of cake. That is, until you consider the full-time job, the family, the house, gym, social events, the snow-shoeing and skiing in the winter, and the biking, camping, and traveling in the summer. With all of those things already on my calendar, a week could slip past me before I found the time to let my mind wander long enough to meld a few pen-stroked circles into eyes, ears, and pot-bellies. A handful of hard deadlines at work and I'd be stumbling home in a daze, wondering how the entire day got away from me without a chance or the energy to scratch out a fuzzy little critter on a scrap of paper. But, I had set the bar and was determined to leap over it.

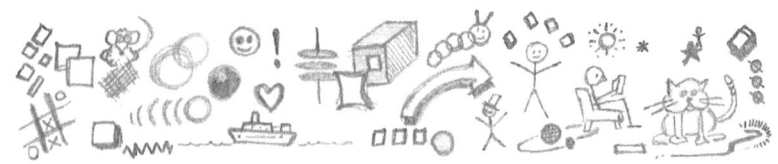

I began to doodle animals when I could during meetings or on weekends, frequently putting them in unrealistic settings or giving them absurd, anthropomorphic qualities. Early on, while I was trying to find some discipline, I would post two in one week or skip a week altogether. Eventually though, I found the rythmn of the process and stuck to one posting per week. The inconsistencies lead to a final number of 59 for the year.

During the year, friends sent me photos of animals, either as inspiration for a new doodle or in response to an existing one, and I posted them with comments. I've included them in this collection, with the photographer's permission, but have not counted those posts toward my year's goal.

Sometimes the animals are angry or sad or hungry, but none of the art is drawn to make the reader unhappy. In other words, while I was drawing, I never expressed my own anger or frustrations through my art. And as for family-friendly, while I was doodling I asked myself if the subject matter could be printed on the comics page of a small town paper without outrage from readers.

In migrating the web postings to a book format, I made some minor changes to some of the text for cohesiveness. You can see the originals, in color, at http://thomphelps.wordpress.com. This book, though, includes full page doodles that you can't find on the web, and some insights into what I was thinking for certain doodles as the months passed.

These drawings are rough—black "roller" pen with gel ink or pencil on low-grade copier paper—because they're just quick doodles. In most cases, one of them would take me fifteen minutes to complete, a minute to scan into my computer, and

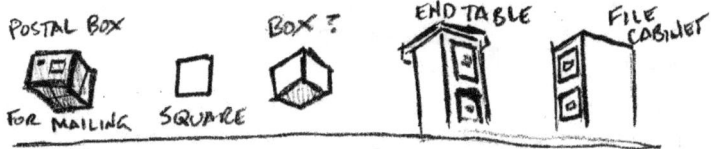

POSTAL BOX   BOX ?   END TABLE   FILE CABINET

FOR MAILING   SQUARE

another 15 or 20 minutes to color using Adobe® Photoshop®. From the brain, to the pen, to the web, in under one hour. Not that there's much brain involved.

Sometimes the pencil drawings took longer, especially the ones I did while camping. But that was because the drawing itself was more of a relaxation exercise, along with going for hikes and taking naps beneath the pine trees. On a camping weekend, I sometimes started a drawing on a Friday afternoon and finished on a Sunday morning, playing with the sketch on and off for 15 minutes here or there.

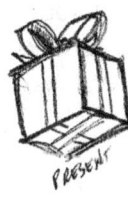

PRESENT

Beyond the satisfaction of posting each drawing and the sense of completion that comes with it, I get great joy from the readers' comments. Almost all of the readers are friends of mine, and it's amazing to see how funny they are when they expand on my basic scenarios. Their comments are the real art in this project, like the "50 ways to leave your lobster" song lyrics that were posted to my doodle of a shrimp walking off with his packed bags. Including them in this collection, though, was beyond the scope of this book, so check out the comments online for an extra chuckle, and feel free to add some of your own.

Merchandising

When I started the Snaring Woodland Creatures blog, I put some of the doodles on merchandise for sale over the internet. I limited the types of merchandise to mugs and t-shirts. Though I did receive one request to print my praying mantis on a pair of thong underwear, I decided to keep to my goal of the entire project being family-freindly.

Interestingly, the very first Snaring Woodland Creature doodle—a welding beaver—was also the first piece of merchandise for sale. It was just a line drawing on a plain white coffee mug. As of the writing of this introduction, that mug has been the most popular of all my Woodland Creature merchandise. People from around the world have purchased them. I like to imagine that somewhere in New Zealand an offshore oil rig welder is sipping tea from a mug adorned with my doodle. Or that I've brought a tiny ray of sunshine into the otherwise boring life of a New York City skyscraper union welder, last name, Beaver.

Draw!

I think it's good for your coordination. It's good for your imagination. It's a great way to work out a problem. Pick up a pencil and draw. It's a fun, stress-releasing exercise. Let your mind wander as the tip of your pen or pencil skates across the lake of paper. There are thousands of doodles inside of you. They just need a door to get out.

Don't feel self-conscious about how good or how bad you draw. If you can't draw a straight line, draw a squiggly one. If you can only draw stick figures, then draw an army of them.

I think doodling is important for everybody, young and old. It connects synapses in young, developing brains and helps make new connections in mature ones. You can draw at any age. If you think you're too old, try doodling next to the crossword puzzle. You've already got the pen and the paper right there and plenty of descriptive suggestions in the crossword clues for subject matter.

I hope you get a kick out of this collection and that it inspires you to doodle now and then.

~ *Thom*

January

The new year is upon me, 2009, and I find myself wanting a new creative outlet. I decide to draw one doodle per week, family-friendly, related to animals, and post them online.

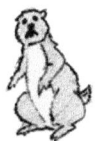

Lodge a complaint

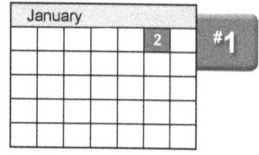

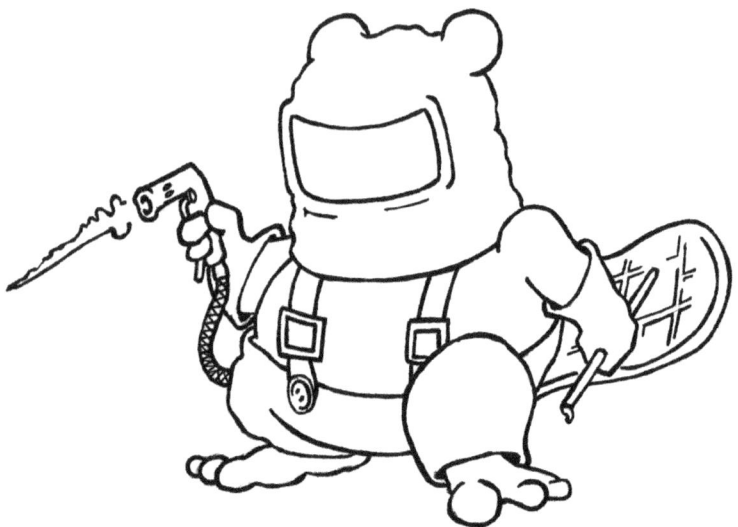

It would be a shame if beavers decided to drop the lumber trade and took up welding. As natural engineers, though, I think the things they built would really stand the test of time.

January   #2

January					
	5				

Aw, nuts

A squirrel has moved into our neighborhood. He runs the fence line and taunts the dogs in their yards, like an angry heckler at a comedy club.

If they get too close, he scampers off, only to return later to chastise and berate them again.

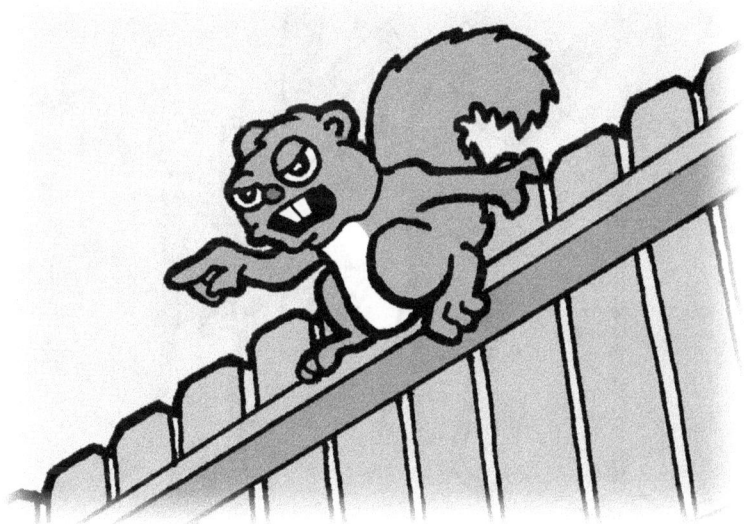

Pray it doesn't come to this

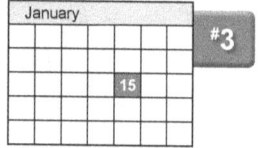

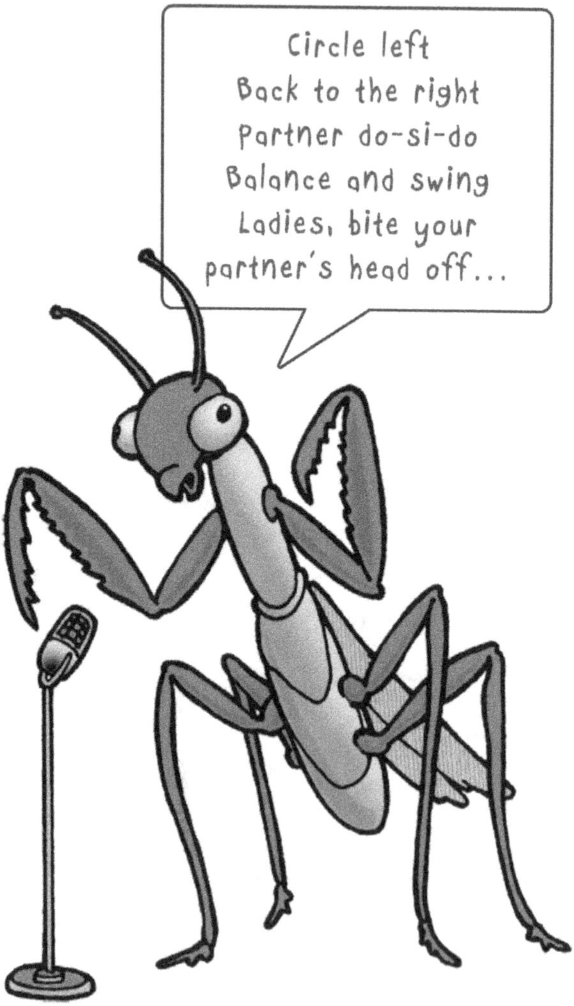

> Circle left
> Back to the right
> Partner do-si-do
> Balance and swing
> Ladies, bite your
> partner's head off...

This is why praying mantises shouldn't call square dances.

Plus, the dance floor gets all slippery.

January #4

16

A rabbit in my back yard

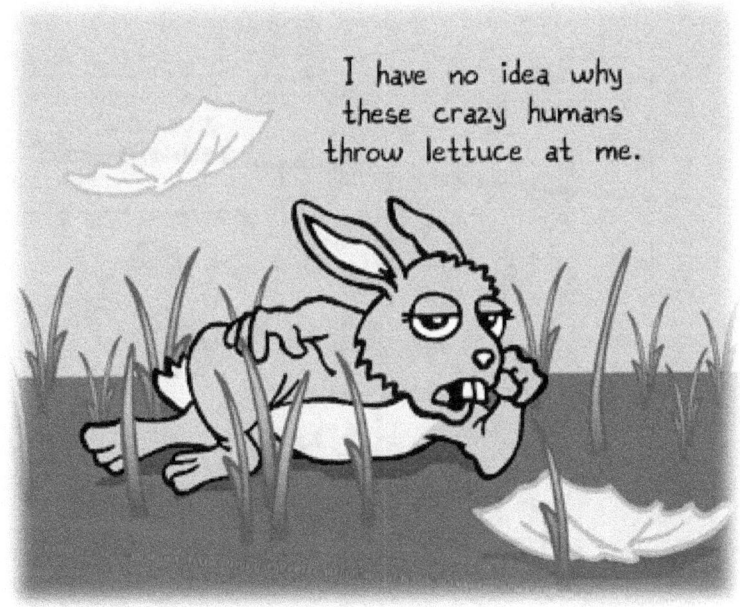

We have several rabbits in our neighborhood. They scurry from yard to yard. It's fun to see their footprints in the snow.

Occasionally, we see one hunkered down in the center of our lawn, curled-up under the butterfly bush, or nibbling on the leaves of the babies' breath it uses as a bed.

We know we're not supposed to, but sometimes we toss them bits of vegetables like carrots and lettuce. They never eat our veggies.

(Never feed or touch wild animals, no matter how cute or cuddly they are. Don't even get close to them.)

Chili's nemesis

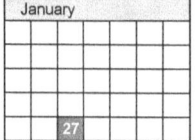

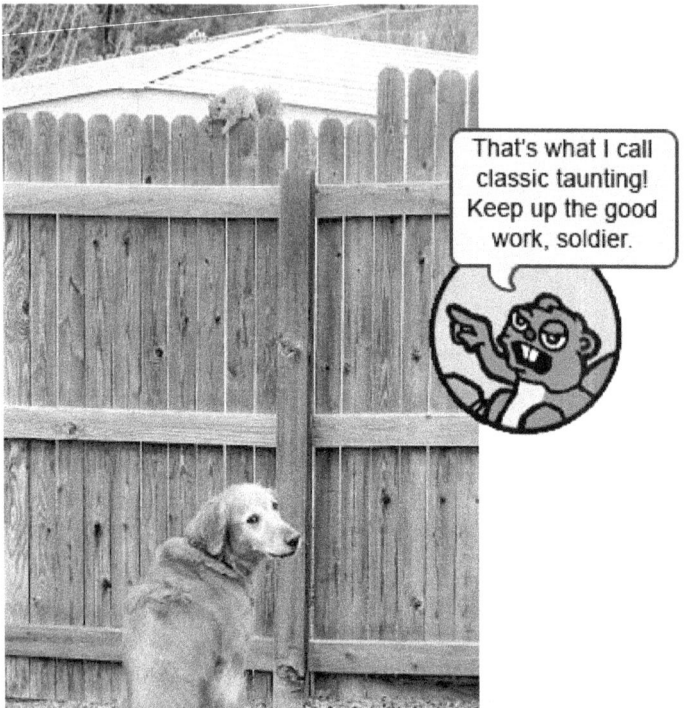

I received a photo of our friend, Chile, in response to "Aw, nuts" that I had to include. Life imitating art.

…Speaking of squirrels, Chile has had an arch enemy his entire adult life. While the squirrel usually just makes a mad dash between houses, on one particular day it decided to stop and taunt Chile. They exchanged chatters and barks for close to 15 minutes. When I went out to try and shoo the squirrel away it just stared at me, with a glazed look in its eyes. To be honest, it scared me, and instead of scaring away the squirrel, I brought Chile inside. I had visions of "Christmas Vacation" with the squirrel lunging for my jugular…

~ Michael

January · #5

27

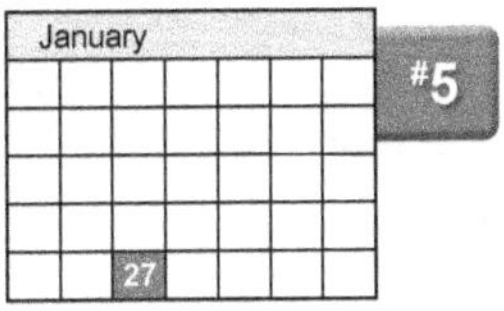

Cannonball!

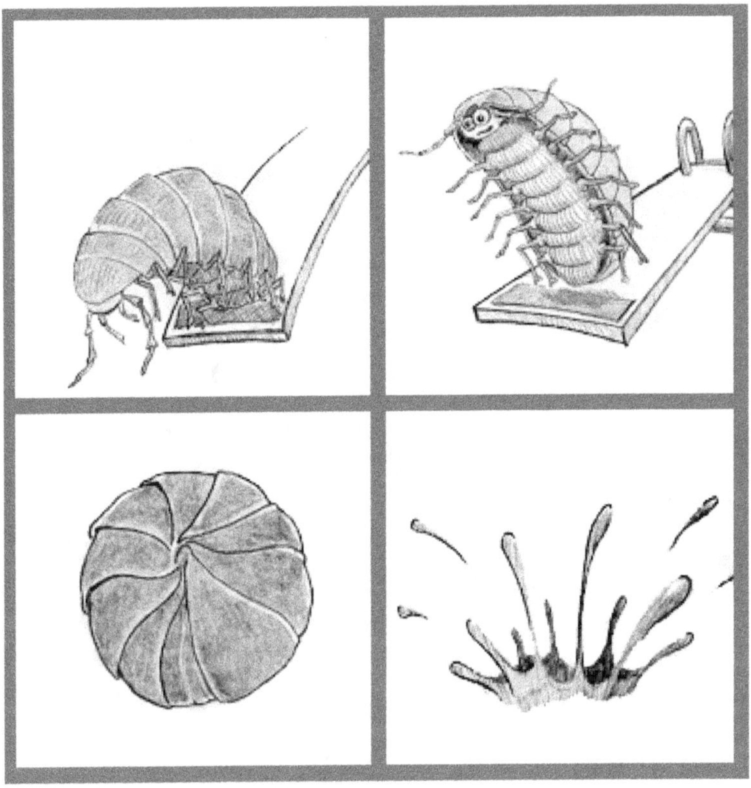

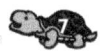

It is cold today. A frigid -3 degrees as I was driving to work. Cold weather makes me think of summertime and fun things you can't do when your nostrils are full of ice, like doing a cannonball into a swimming pool.

In the animal kingdom, I think the most perfect cannonballs would be performed by the roly poly. Our pill bug friend is uniquely designed for maximum cannonballitude.

Second place: the armadillo.

eyes

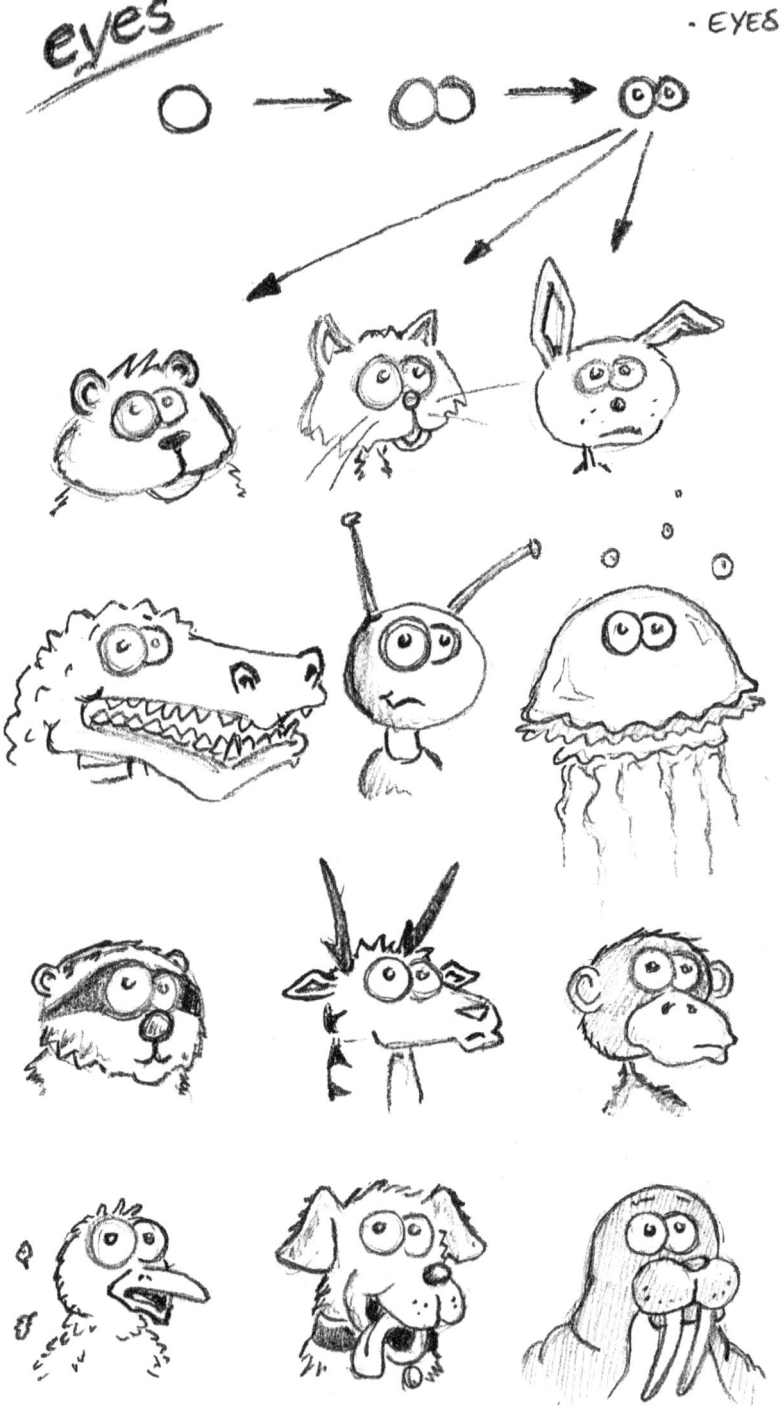

February

I'm finding my pace. The roly poly doing a cannonball
into the swimming pool was a lot of fun to draw.
I'm starting to get comfortable again with the feel of
the pencil, pressure control and shading, and don't
necessarily feel obligated to convert a pencil drawing
to ink.

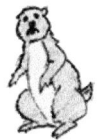

Speaking of armadillos

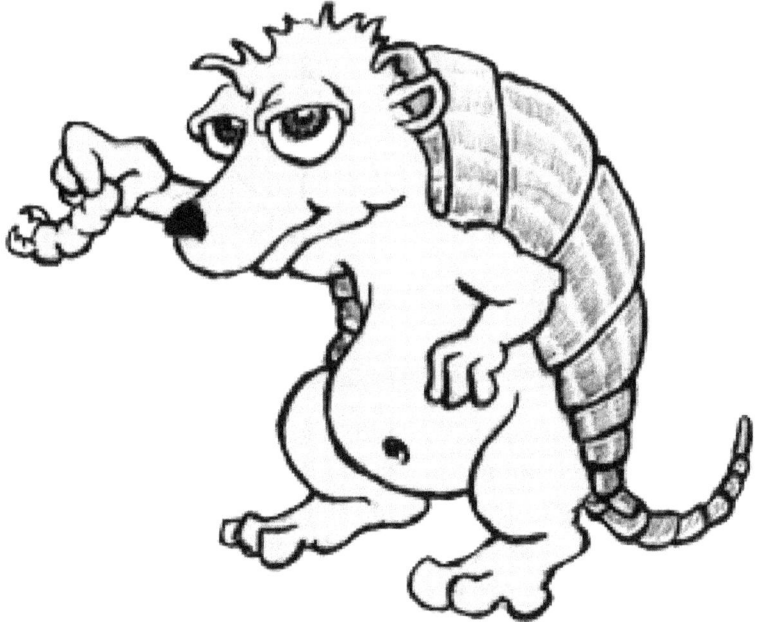

I flew to Austin, Texas at Christmas and drove from Austin to Houston and back while I was there. During all that time on the road I think I only saw one armadillo. When I was growing up there, I saw them all the time.

A classmate and I had a comic strip in the school paper when I was in college called, "Waller City Limits." It was modelled after Berk Breathed's Bloom County and featured an armadillo as the main character. He looked an awful lot like this little fellow. Same stance and facial expression.

February

10

#7

There's a new one in town

Prairie dogs live in prairie dog towns.

Do they have official jobs?

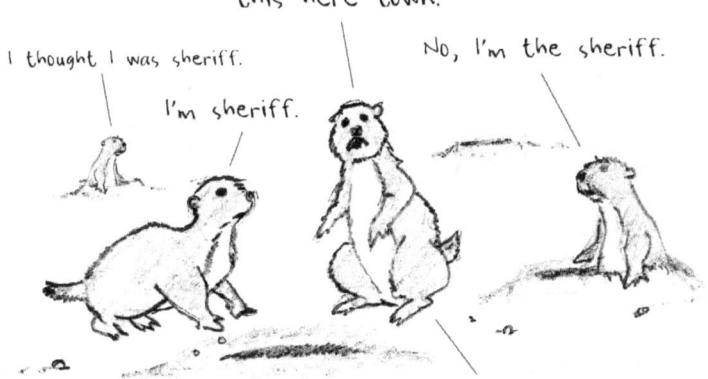

Kids these days

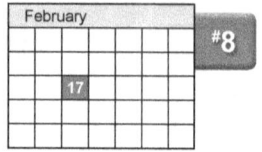

Next to puppies and kittens, baby goats and sheep are probably the cutest, most playful woodland creatures on the planet. I love to watch them chasing each other, mock head-butting and standing, perfectly balanced, on all manner of things.

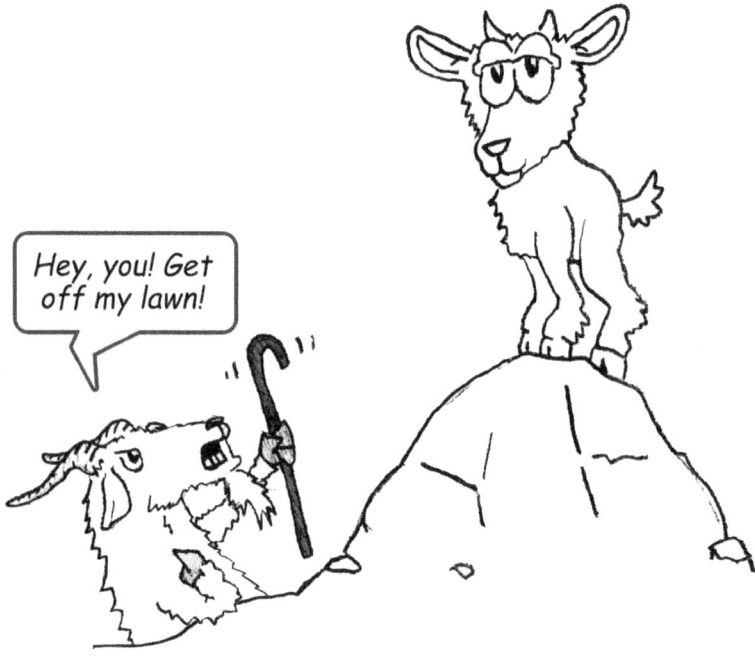

My wife had a pair of goats when she was young who would climb on her mother's car and perch on the edge of the chrome, walking only along the narrow edges of the car's windshield and frame.

Sometimes when they get older, billy goats tend to get gruff.

February | #9

24

Animal social clubs

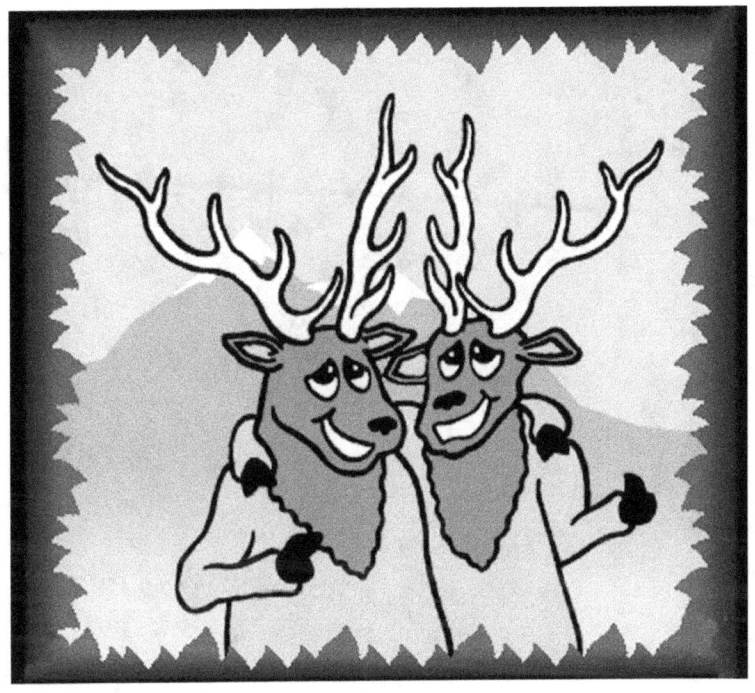

If we have an elk's club, what do elks have?

Do moose hang out in a human lodge one weekend a month to plan charitable fundraisers and to let their hair down?

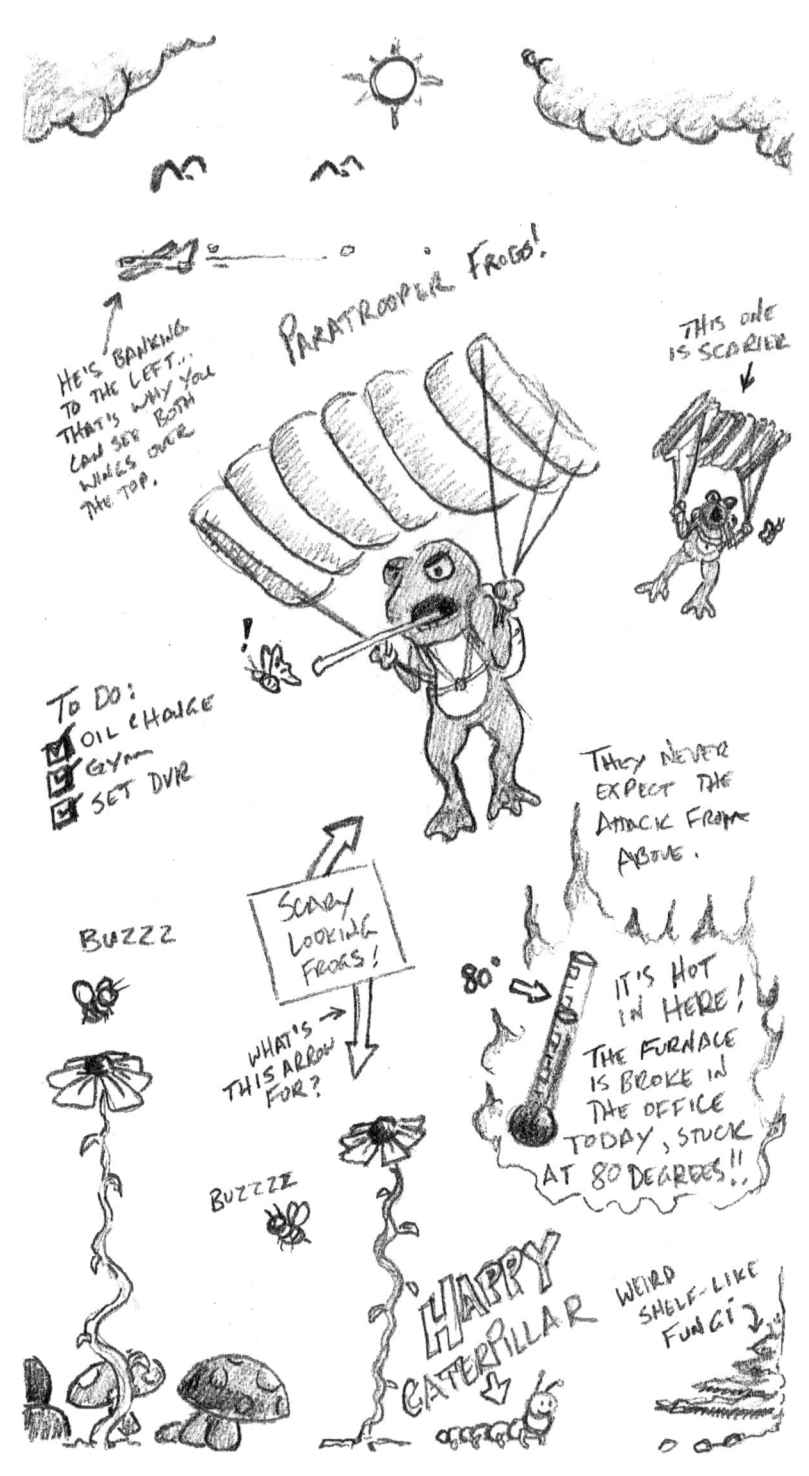

March

I never know where my doodles are going to take me.
Sometimes they just organize my thoughts or help me
vent the frustrations of the day. Other times I find
them creating a world where parachuting frogs swoop
down on unsuspecting butterflies.

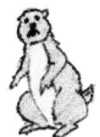

Say it with me:

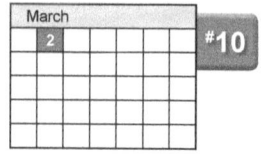

Everything's better with monkeys!

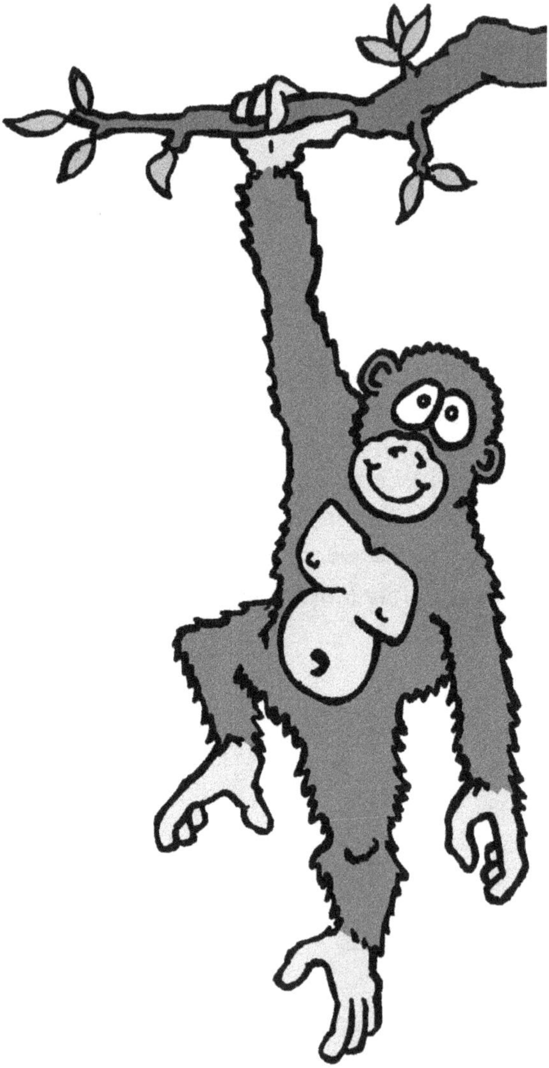

Dauber or dobber?

There's a kind of wasp in the South called a mud dauber. It builds its home out of mud by "daubing" little bits at a time with its jaws.

I imagine a southern insect to be a tough, contemplative bug of few words.

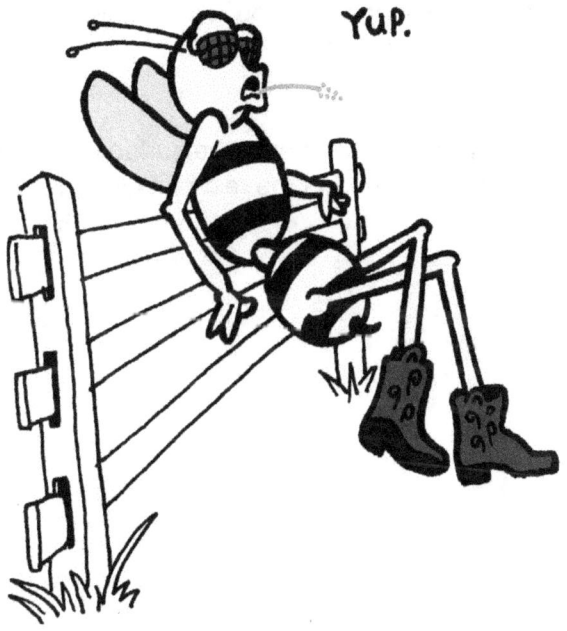

For some reason, I always picture them leaning against split-rail fences.

peek-a-boo

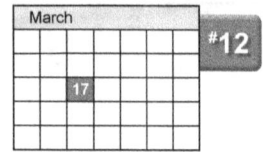

So, you come upon a pair of eyes staring up at you from the water.

What could they belong to? A frog? An alligator? A mudskipper fish? A crocodile? A toad?

Do you dare slip your head under the surface of the water and take a peak to see what the rest of it looks like?

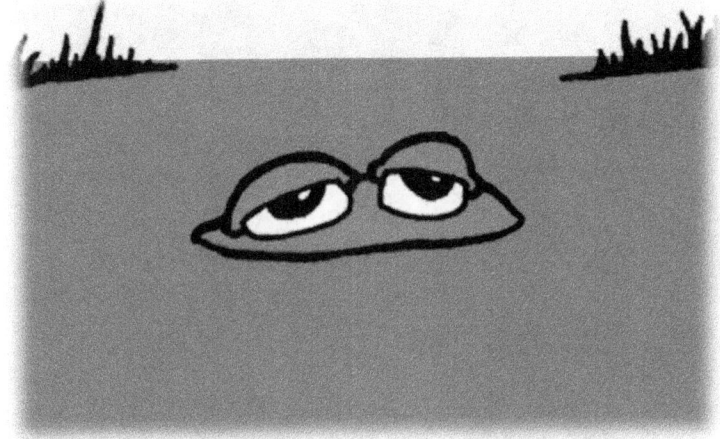

A frog would be too easy

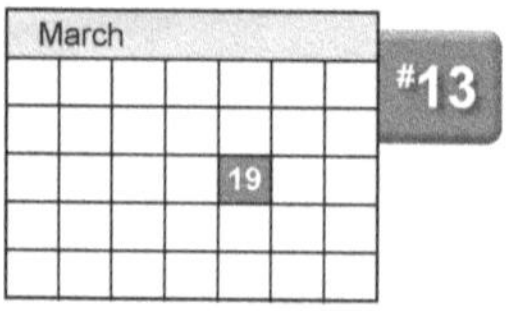

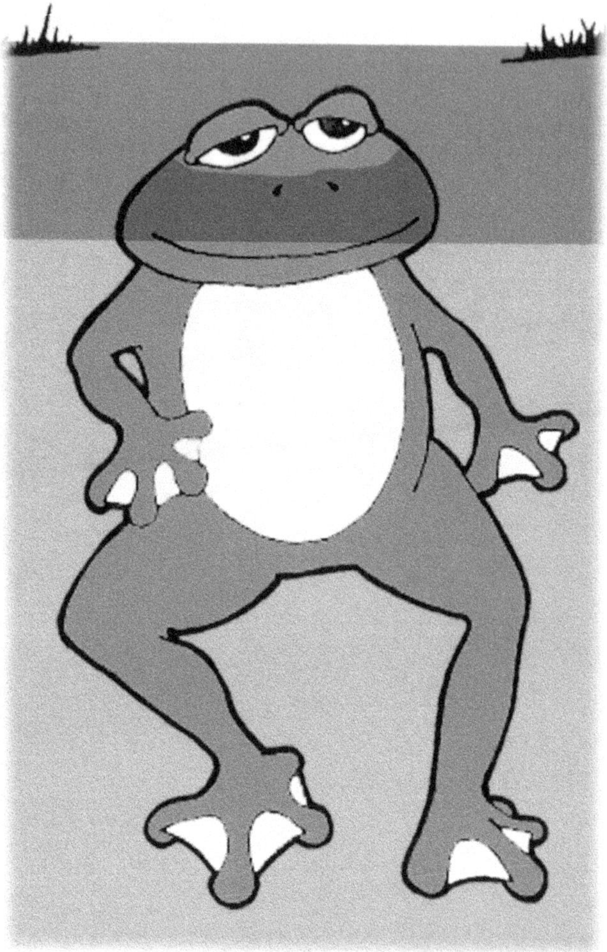

It could have been anything, I guess, but frogs are easy to draw. I like how she's kind of suspended, floating in the water.

Plus I like her feet.

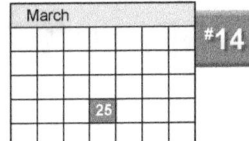

Once again with FEELING!

Everything's better with monkeys!

In a production meeting today, we were brainstorming ideas on the dry-erase board and someone tossed out the idea "space monkey." Well, that needed a doodle to go along with it. So here it is:

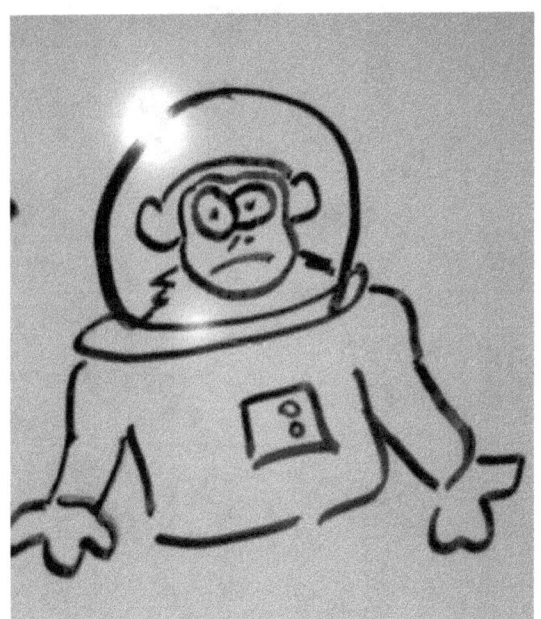

Do ants dance?

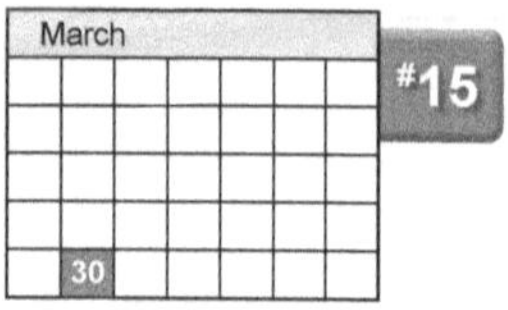

March

#15

30

I was in a meeting, doodling as usual to stay focused, and my little circles became bugs, then ants, and finally ants dancing. It reminded me of a song my friend, Judy Feeney, put out a couple years ago called "The Ants Dance".

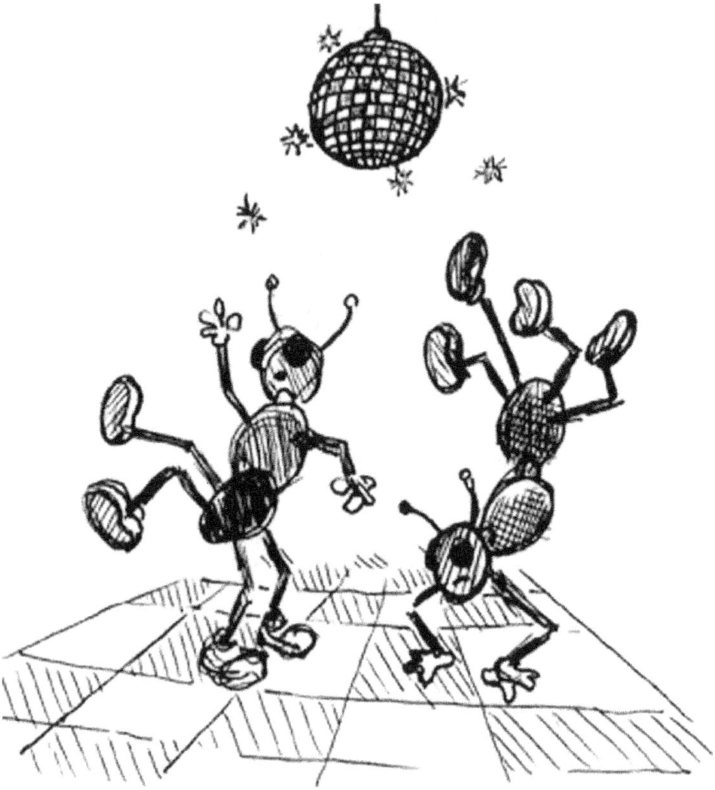

If ants dance, what style is more popular with them? I'd guess line dancing or maybe salsa.

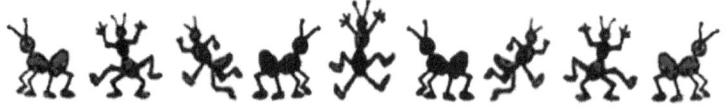

Go to: www.judyfeeney.com

April

I can feel the change in the air: spring has sprung, though it doesn't look like it yet (it is Colorado after all) what with the snow on the ground. But the rabbits in my yard are out in force, birds are returning, and bees have begun their flitting.

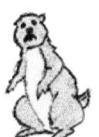

When bees act out

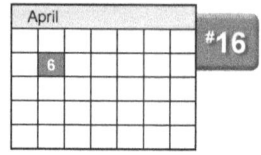

To bee or not to bee, that is the question;

Whether 'tis nobler in the hive to suffer

The stings and stingers of outrageous fortune,

Or to take wing against a sky of troubles,

And by opposing, end them. To die, to sleep;

No more...

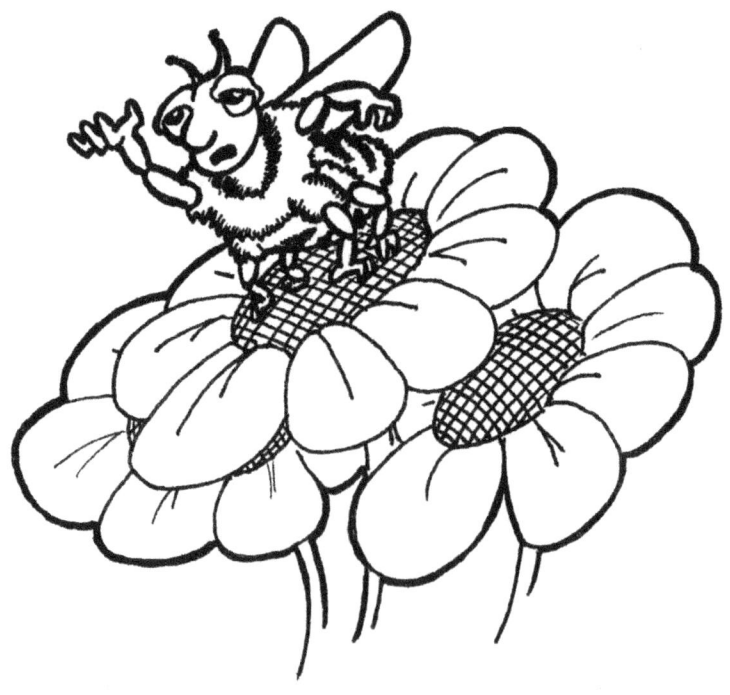

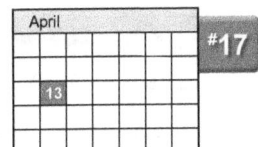

Spikey, dazed and confused

Hedgehogs are so cute, all pointy-nosed, soft-bellied and spikey on the back. When you look at them straight on, they have this bewildered, dazed look.

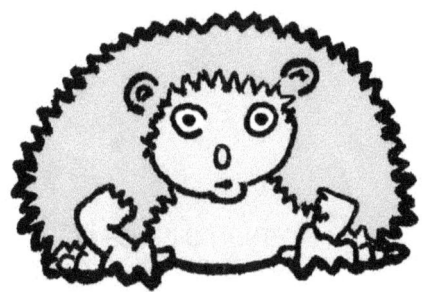

But when I stand one up, he looks an awful lot like an armadillo (February). Even the same arm position, belly button and feet.

I really need to broaden my styles a bit.

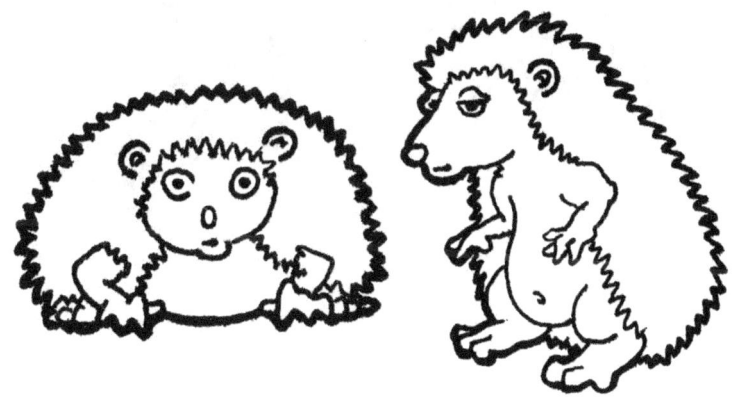

Eek! A cockroach!

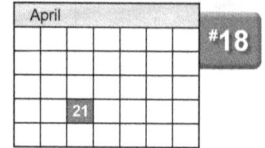

People have been saying for years that since cockroaches have lasted so long (tens of millions of years), they can survive anything we dish at them.

I wonder what *they're* saying?

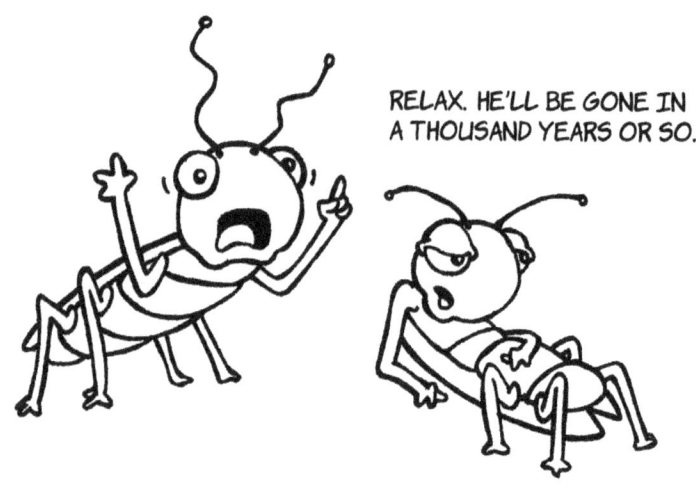

THAT HUMAN HAS BEEN TRYING TO CRUSH ME FOR HOURS! IT'S STARTING TO FREAK ME OUT!

RELAX. HE'LL BE GONE IN A THOUSAND YEARS OR SO.

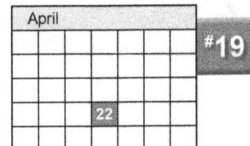

Thom Phelps

Earth Day

It's like Valentine's Day for me. 19 years ago, my wife and I had our first real kiss. It was at an Earth Day concert in Austin.

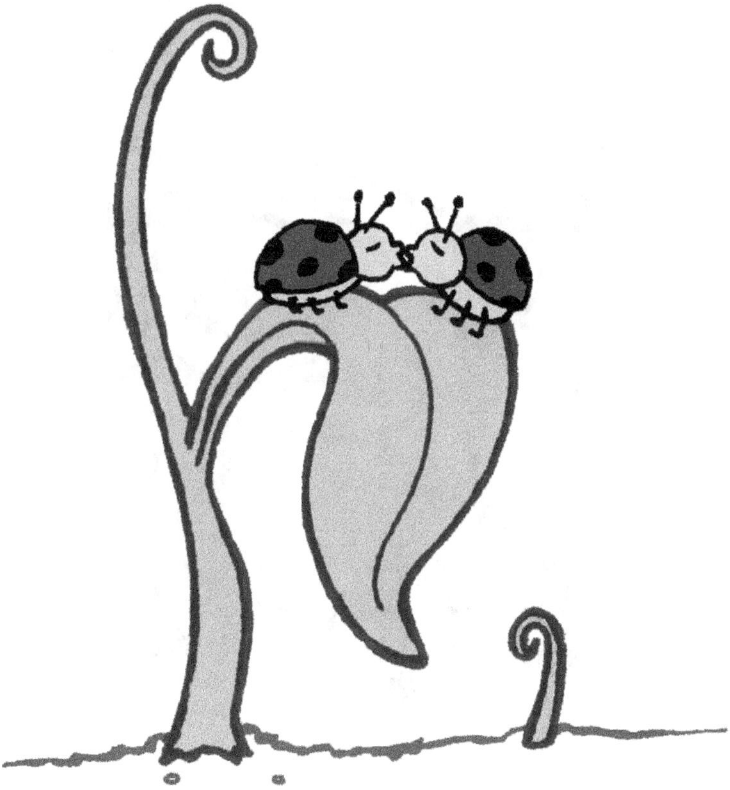

This little piggy

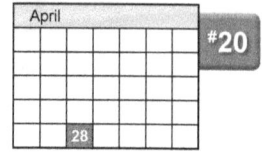

…had roast beef. (You can tell by his full belly and content smile.)

All the news this week about swine flu got me thinking about our porcine pals. They've always got a smile on their faces, even if they are looking down their noses at us.

Maybe they just like to ham it up?

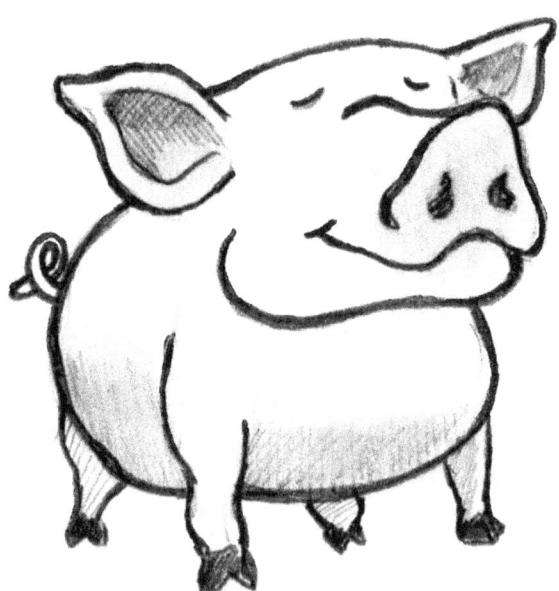

May

This month, Michele Norris interviewed the cartoonist and children's book author, Moe Willems, on NPR's *All Things Considered* about getting adults to draw. It was a fascinating discussion that cemented my belief in the importance of doodling. Hearing them talk about kids giving up drawing once they realize they're not good enough to be professionals saddened me and reinforced my enthusiasm for this project.

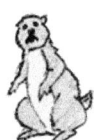

a Turtle

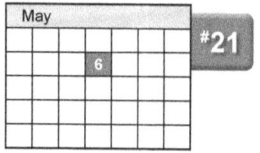

When I was very young, some cousins of mine in Phoenix had a box turtle as a pet. (Maybe it was some kind of tortoise?) It wandered their yard, ever so slowly and seemed so huge to me. I was about seven years old at the time, so I'm sure it was actually pretty small.

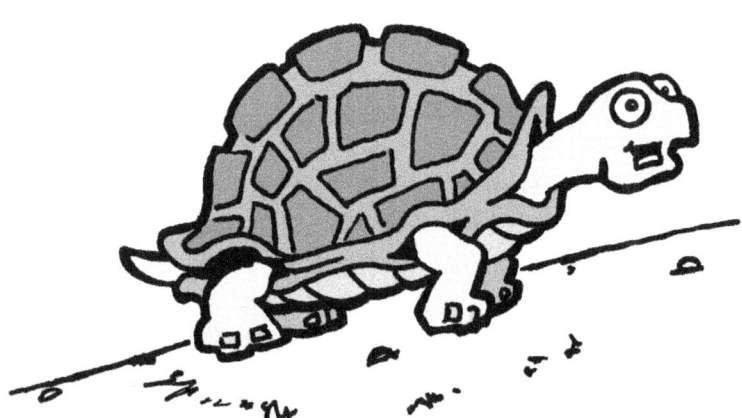

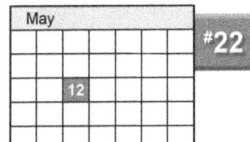

Moray eels are magnificent

A friend of mine went to the aquarium with his daughter and saw a moray eel. Then he drew it with chalk on the concrete when they were home and sent me the photo.

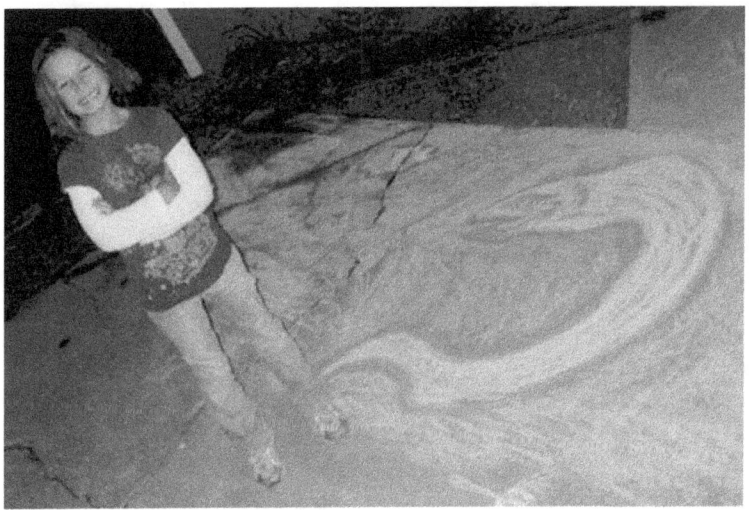

I followed suit with a cartoon version.

It's hard to make a moray eel look friendly without it ending up looking like a slow-witted dinosaur (like this one).

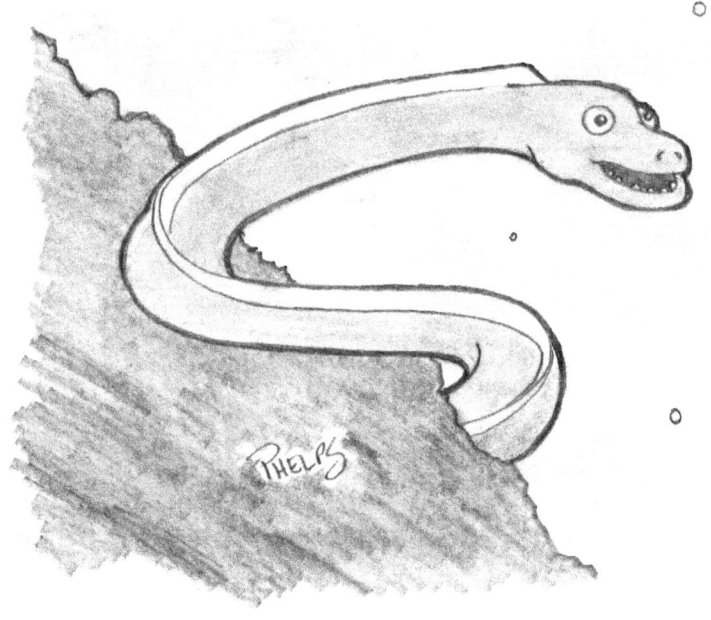

When drawing eels and sea snakes, you can always start by drawing an S or a C since they're floating in water.

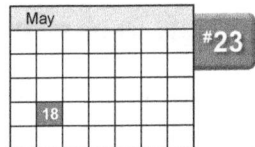

#23

Slower than a sleeping snail

… able to eat bushels of leaves in a single, monotonously slow gulp.

It seems to me that some species wouldn't benefit much from having a super hero among them. Can you get any slower? I wonder if his super power would be to hang from a branch for weeks at a time. Or to stare. The colorful cape would be a nice accessory, though.

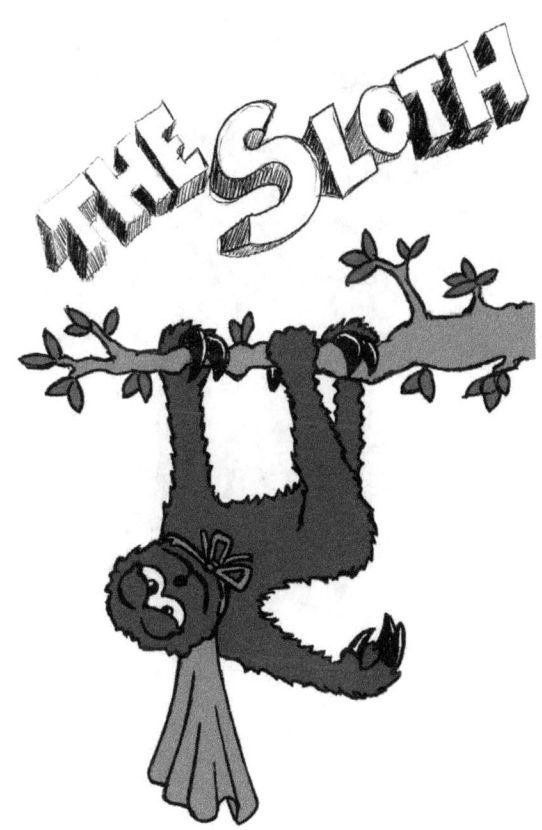

Slow Moose Ahead

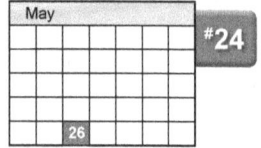

They're already in the middle of the road, making us have to brake anyway. Might as well put those woodland creatures to work.

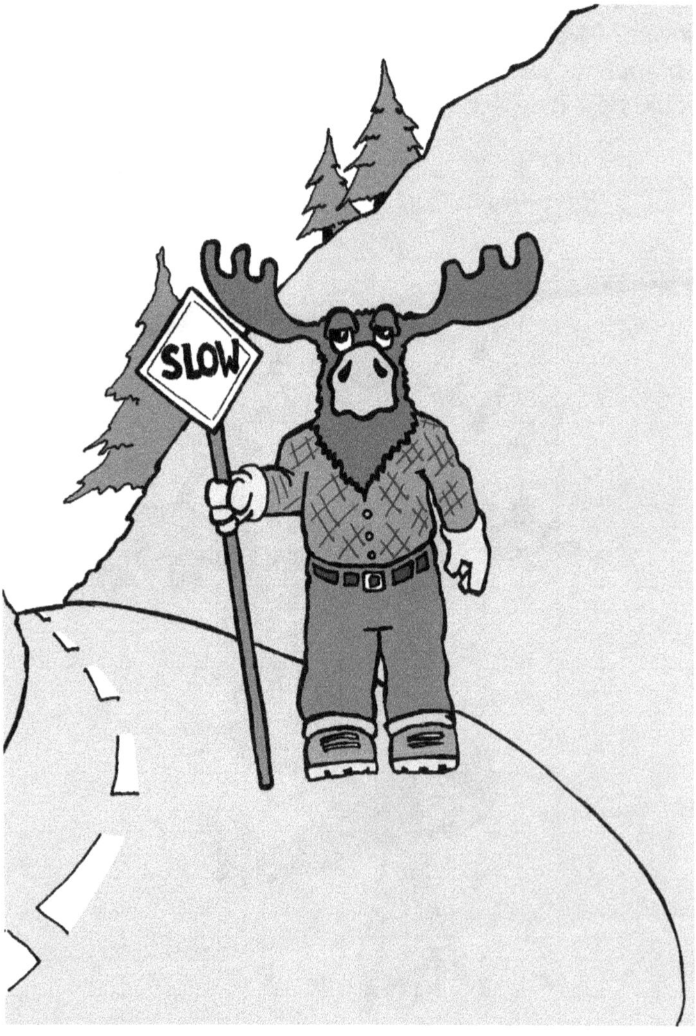

June

Time to air out the tent, replenish the fuel for the camp stove, make sure no critters have decided to turn my packed-away sleeping bags into cozy homesteads. In other words, it's time to start camping!

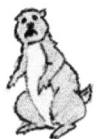

What came first

June

			3			

#25

the chicken or the egg?

The coffee! Coffee always comes first.

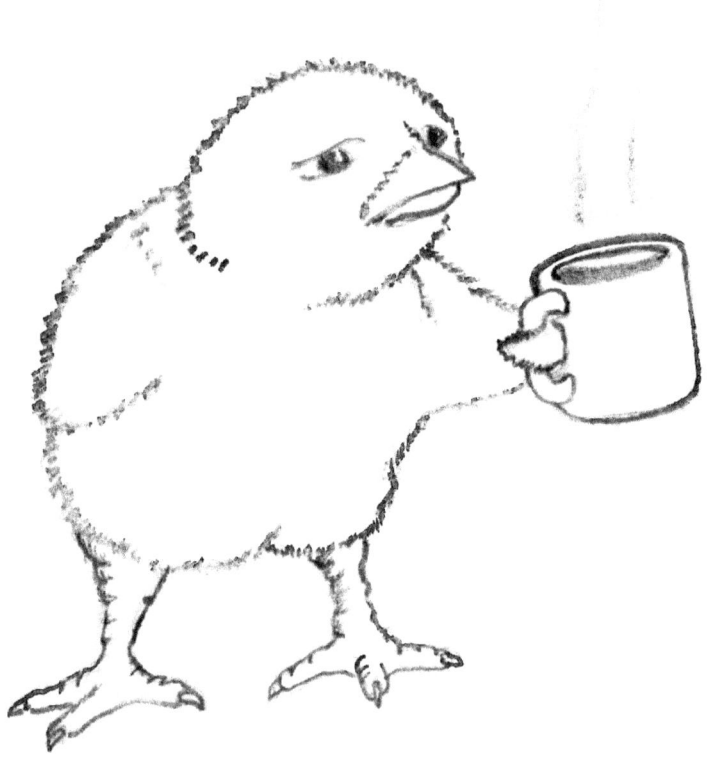

June
#26

9

A question of metrics

What do Europeans call an inch worm?

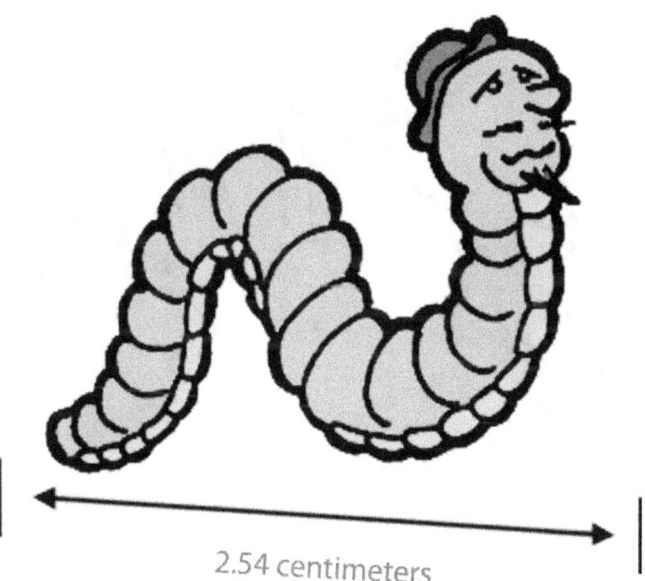

2.54 centimeters

The lizard brain

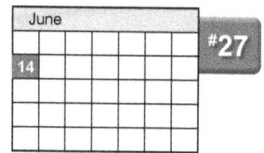

Reptile brains only process the basic fundamentals.

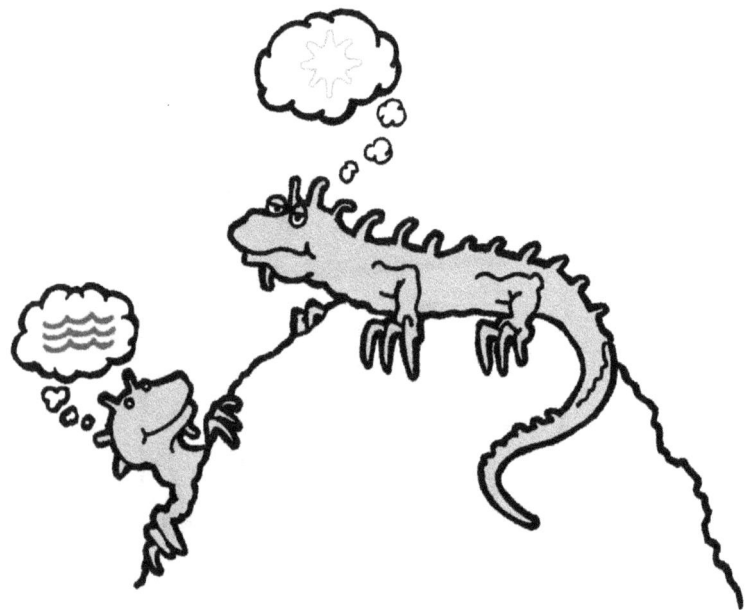

Translation:

"Hey, Keanu, let's go for a dip in the surf!"

"Thanks, dude, but I just want to soak in some UVs here in the sun."

June						
		18				

Angry iguana

My friend sent this note and photograph. It's a funny coincidence that while I was drawing iguanas in Santa Fe, New Mexico, she was petting wild iguanas in Venezuela!

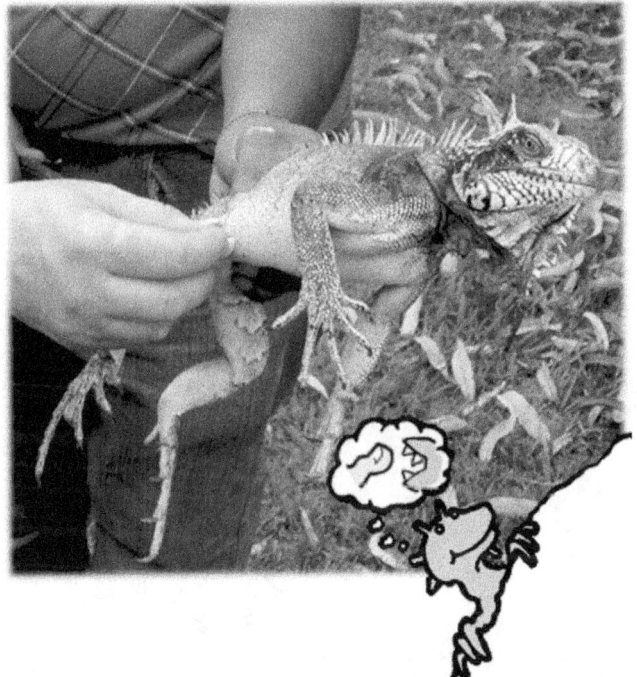

Thought you'd all enjoy these pics from my trip [to Venezuela]. My cousins spotted this iguana in a mango tree. So my uncle climbed the tree and shook him out. I like the angry look on the iguana's face. Right after the last picture was taken, the iguana got his revenge by biting our friend who's petting him by his head. He honestly probably needed stitches on his little finger but the Venezuelan answer for that was more beer and dancing.

~ Ely

Never handle wild animals.

Squirrel in the sky

June
	23				

My scanner is broken this week, which means my hand-drawn doodles are piling up on my desk. So while I wait for the trusty repair men to do their magic, I'll resort to finding woodland creatures someplace other than my sketch pad. First place to look: out my office window.

There's a cloud that looks suspiciously like a squirrel. I wonder if he's taunting any cloud dogs?

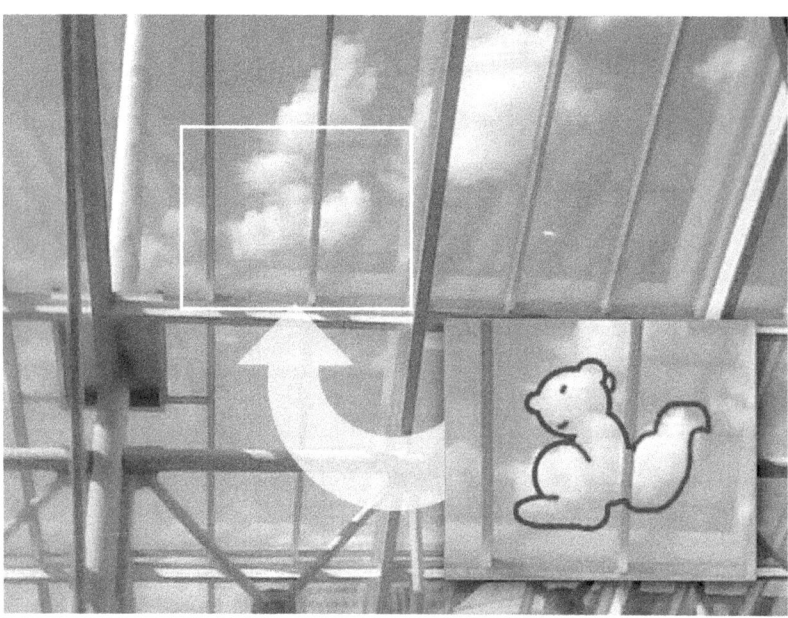

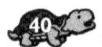

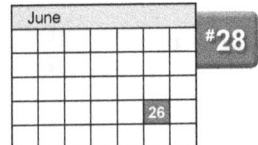

Madame Dungeness sees all

Do animals that typically get classified as an "all you can eat" food ever risk going to a fortune teller?

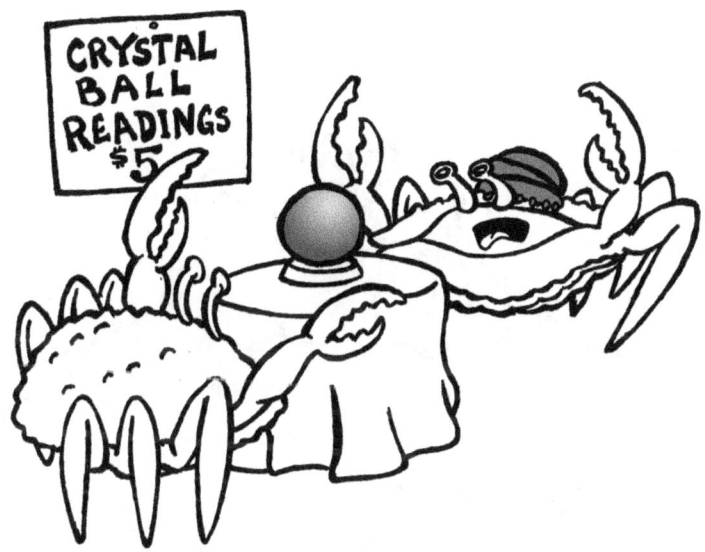

I see an ad campaign in your future for a national restaurant chain. And butter. Lots and lots of garlic butter.

Lazy summer day

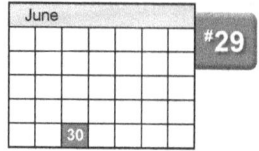

I like the squat, warty shape of this toad, content on his toad stool. A fun doodle.

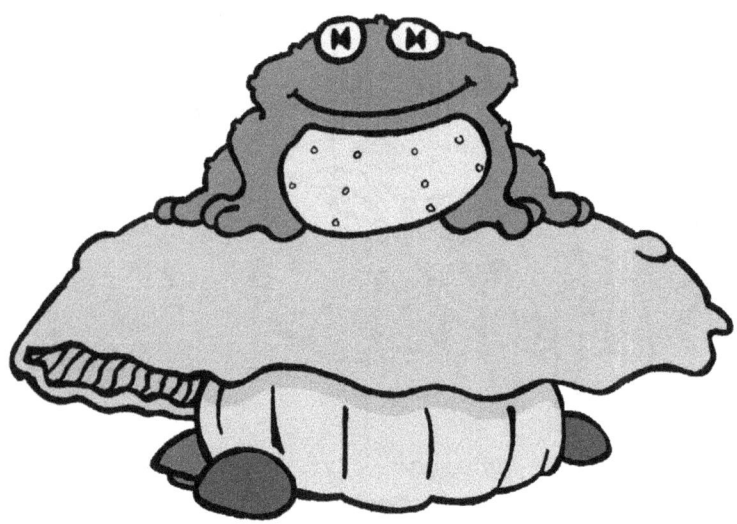

July

Bigger, multi-part doodles are the thrust of this month. Not intentionally. They just appeared organically. Plus an idea for a mutton-chopped children's character.

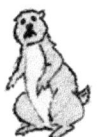

Mutton Chops Make the Dandy Rhino

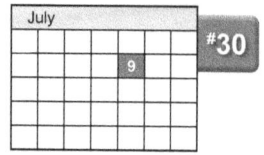

I went camping two weeks ago with friends, among whom was a certain, adorable, most imaginative three-year-old named Ella.

Through suggestions and corrections (number of horns, flatness of forehead) she guided me in sketching some new characters, foremost being Abraham Hornswoggle. He's the dashing fellow in mutton chops, sporting the top hat, cummerbund and cane.

He loves the opera, Sunday walks in the park, and discussing fine art and politics with his dandy friends.

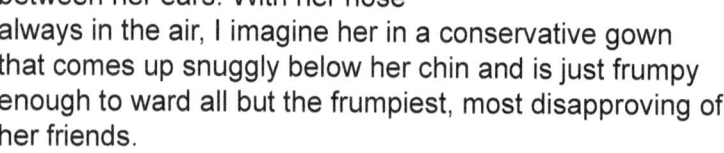

Next up was his disapproving Aunt Sophia. You can tell that she is a "she" by her eyelashes and the bow between her ears. With her nose always in the air, I imagine her in a conservative gown that comes up snuggly below her chin and is just frumpy enough to ward all but the frumpiest, most disapproving of her friends.

In Aunt Sophia's house lives a boarder mouse named Ella who has run of the kitchen pantry and helps with the daily chores. On her free time she roams the expansive garden, finding adventure among the gladiolas and sage.

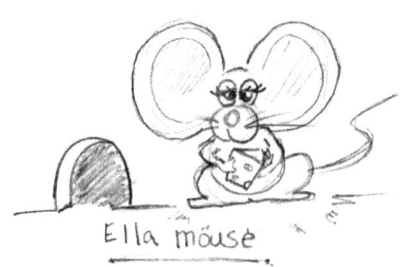

Ella mouse

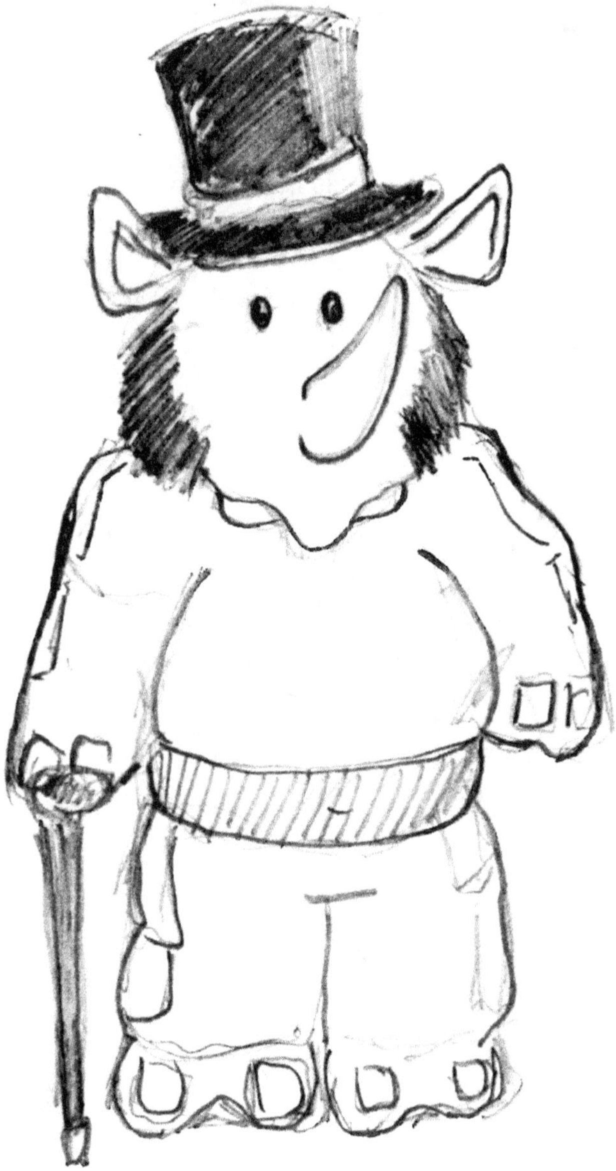

Many thanks to Miss Ella for helping me doodle these creatures.

Plumage

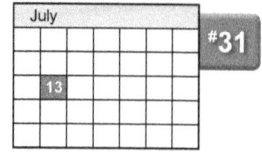

A bird's plumage often reflects its location.

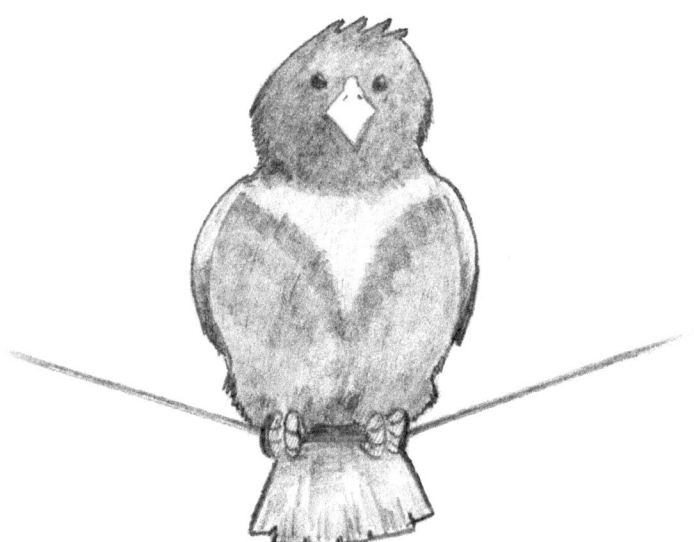

For example, this fellow could be found at a renaissance festival:

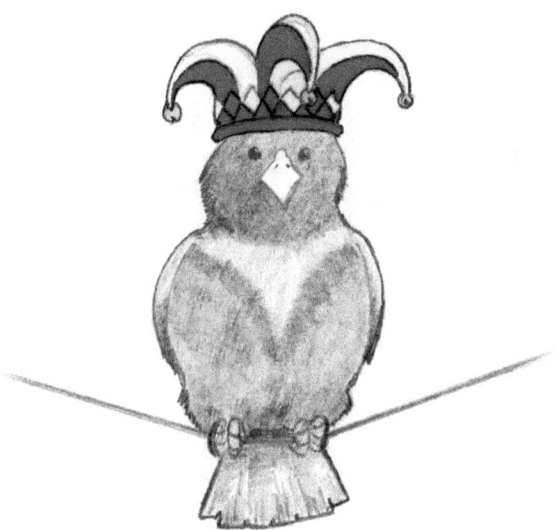

Above the canals of Venice:

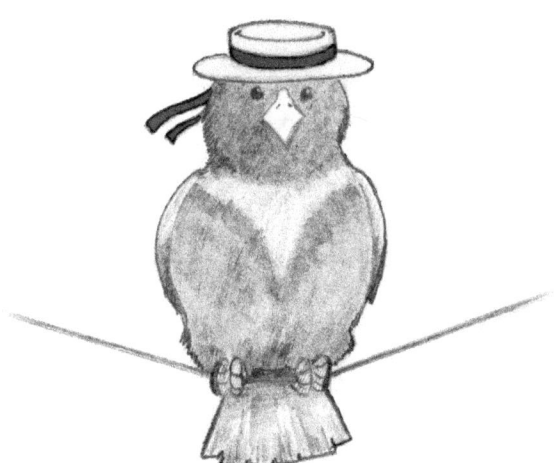

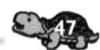

20,000 leagues beneath the sea:

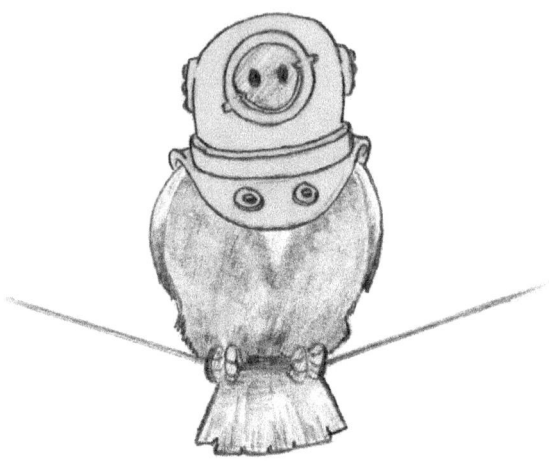

Near an English chocolate factory:

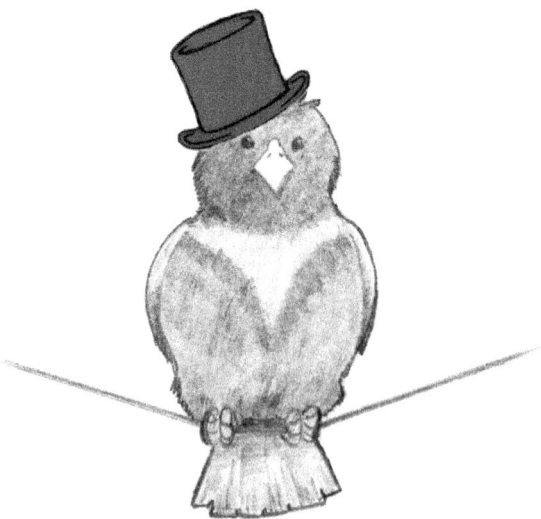

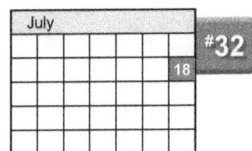

Tea time in the park

Here's Abraham in the park, as mentioned before, enjoying a spot of tea.

I think the owl is part of a small cluster of bad influence characters that occasionally pester Abraham and try to get him to do bad things. He's above their influence, of course.

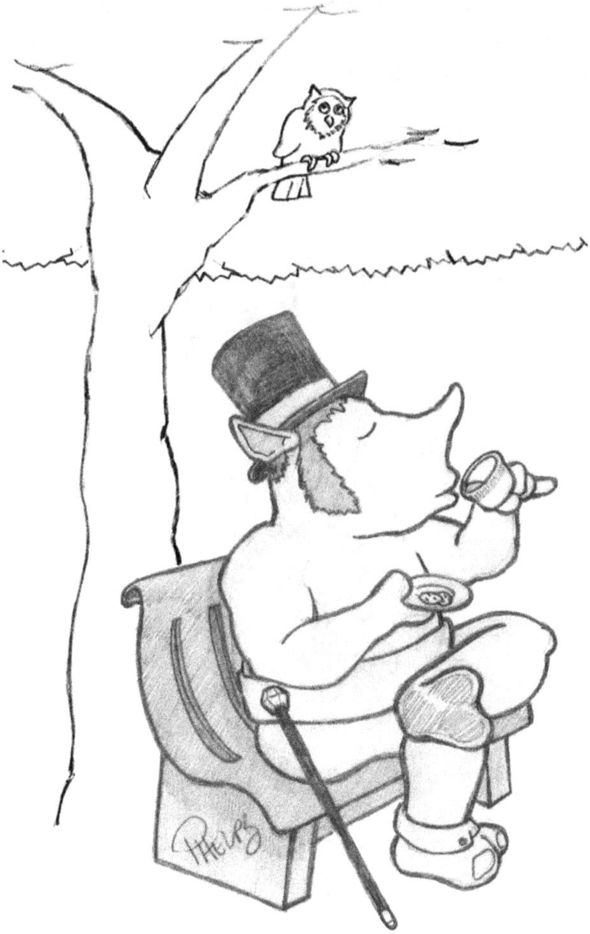

Blue-toed bug

July						
						#33
	21					

Some friends nicknamed their infant son, Benjamin, "Bug." As in, he's cute as a bug.

Recently, while getting artsy and craftsy, they dipped his tiny feet in blue baby paint to make some imprints. Once done, getting the paint off was more of a challenge than they expected and they've been finding little traces of blue in the cracks between his toes ever since. (Just thinking about having paint scrubbed out from between my toes gives me the tickle monster shivers.)

Needless to say, "Bug" became "Bug Blue Toe" for a while. Sounds kind of like a pirate name.

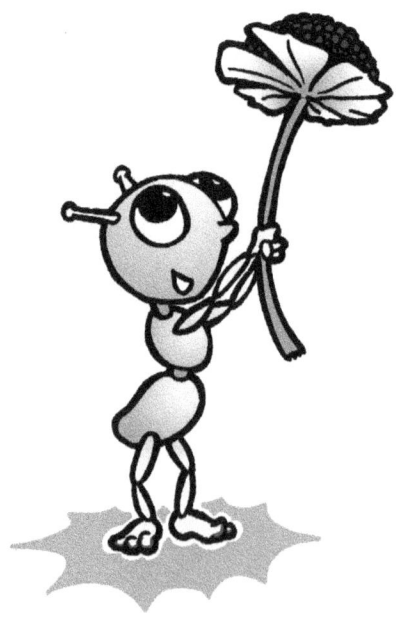

Added trivia: while I was drawing this, I was listening to ELO's "Boy Blue" on my iPod.

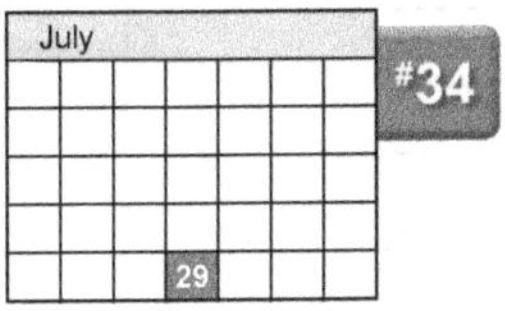

July

#34

Paul

Thom Phelps

29

51

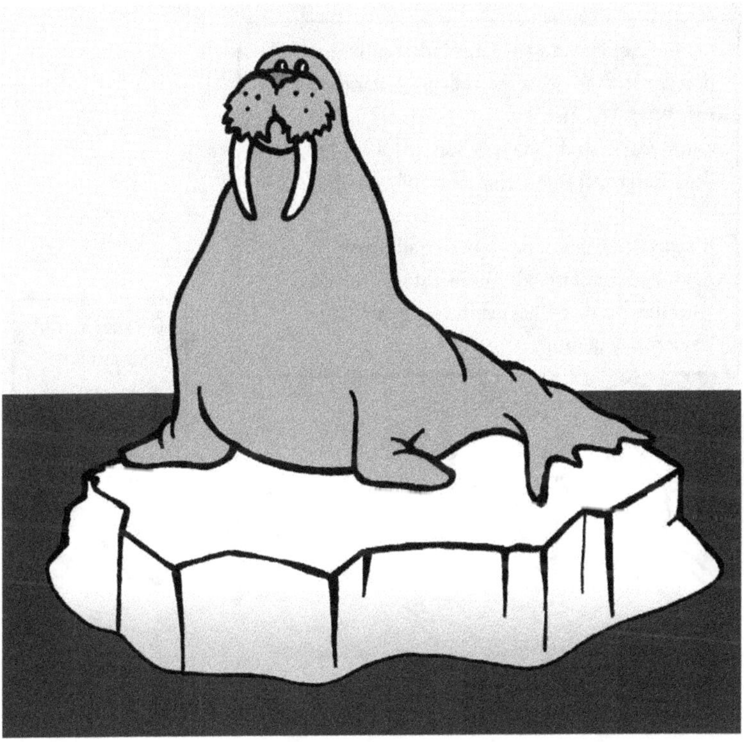

Name calling

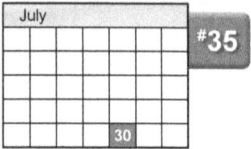

I don't get it. I mean, I'm neither a kangaroo nor a rat. And yet they call me a kangaroo rat. Why, because I've got big feet? I don't drink water and I have a furry, tufted tail, but they don't call me a camel gerbil, do they?

It's just not fair. I'm a seed-gathering nocturnal rodent, who lives underground. It would be more accurate to call me a hamster chipmunk.

Or they could call you a mole mouse!

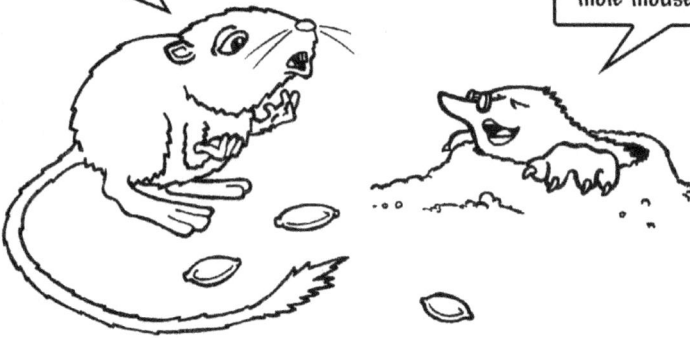

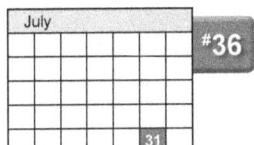

#36

Leaf cutters and wood carvers

Do you think a leaf cutter ant appreciates a finely-grown leaf the way a woodcraftsmen appreciates a beautiful tree?

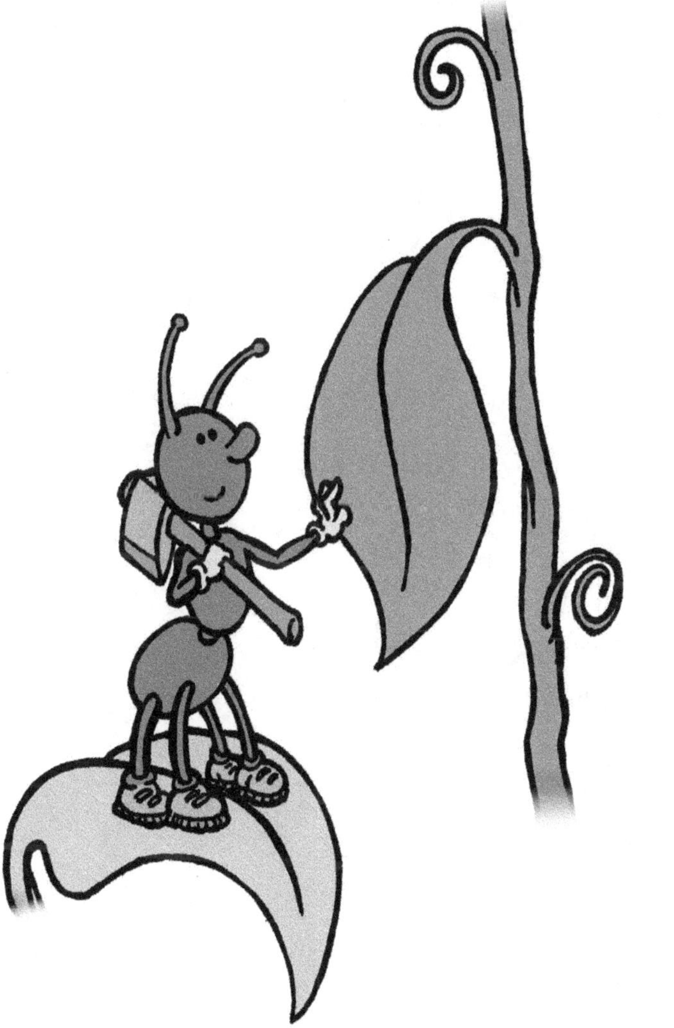

DOGS

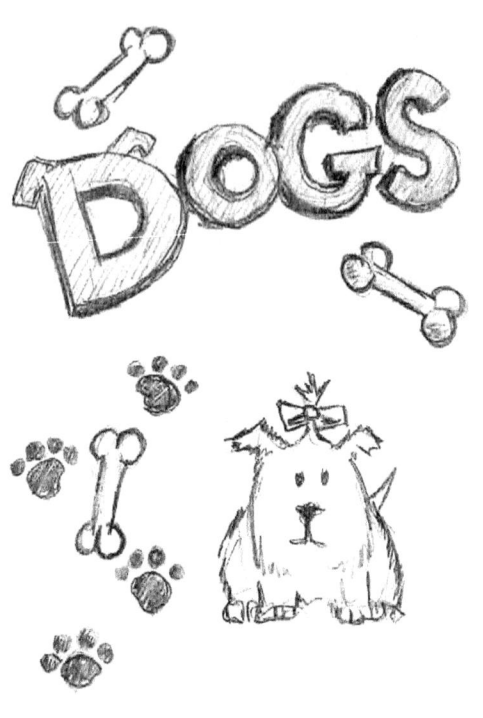

DOODLING DURING A BUMPY AIRPLANE RIDE TO DURANGO IS HARD!!

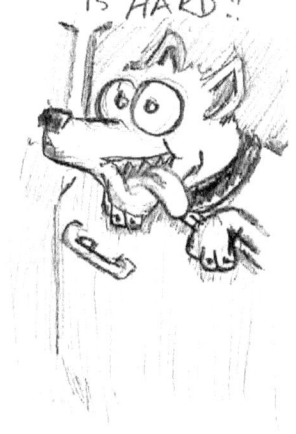

ARE WE STILL IN KANSAS?

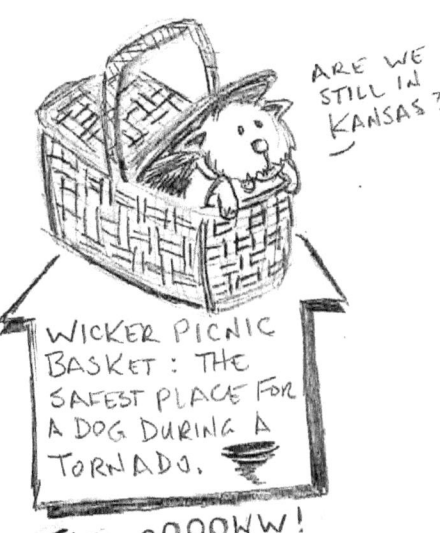

WICKER PICNIC BASKET: THE SAFEST PLACE FOR A DOG DURING A TORNADO.

oooooooww!

DRAWING YOUR TYPICAL "DOG'S BONE":

FOUR CIRCLES, TWO ON EACH SIDE, STACKED LIKE EIGHTS. THEN CONNECT WITH TWO LINES AND ERASE WHERE THEY OVERLAP.

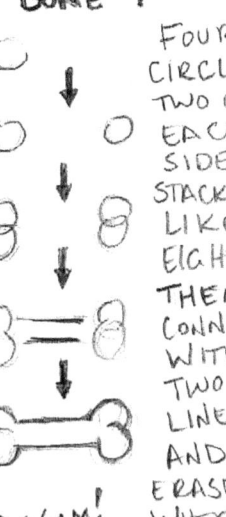

YUM!

August

Except for one large pencil drawing I did over a camping weekend, I was back to doodling with the pen in August. Thick, solid lines and little or no depth of color or angled light source. Kind of like an August day: bright sun shining straight down, casting minimal shadows and washing out colors to their bare essentials.

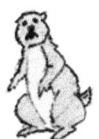

ME! ME! ME! ME! ME!

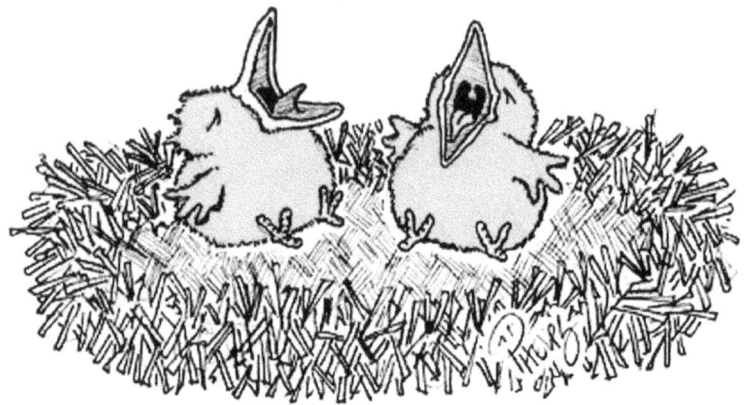

Ungrateful children. "I'm hungry. I'm cold. I'm uncomfortable."

It is the nature of things. When we're little we think the world revolves around us because our brains are developing and we're still being guarded by our parents. Plus, it is a fundamental survival instinct. It's a good thing.

One of the greatest gifts a parent can give a child, though, is a sense of self-reliance and confidence to make it in the world on their own.

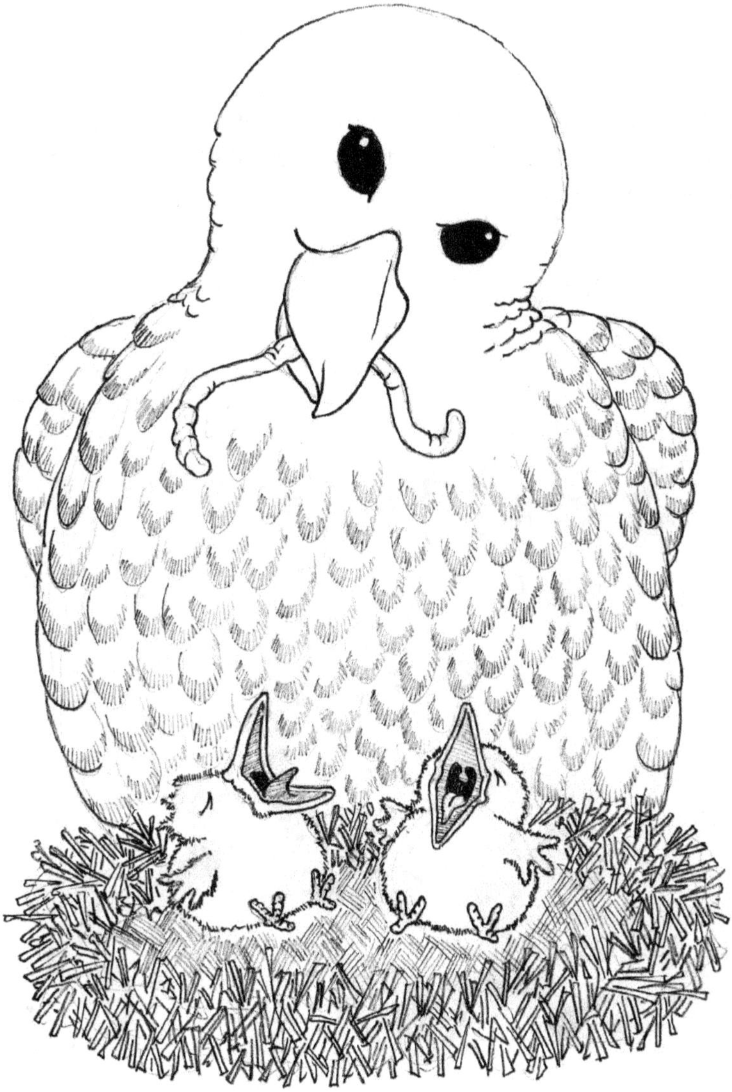

Thom Phelps

Look, ma, no hands!

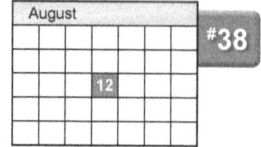

Who doesn't like to dangle from a tree limb or collapse in a pile of leaves and pretend to be dead? If only for a little while, it's fun to play possum.

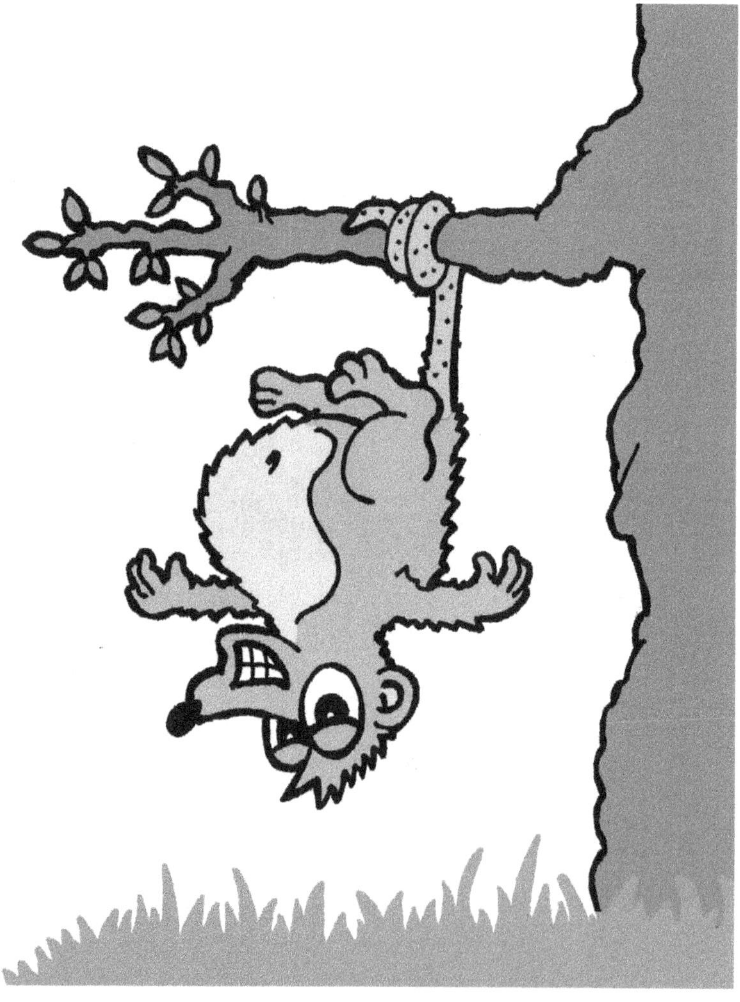

Thom Phelps

August						
						#39
17						

Oodles of Poodle Doodles

Well, not oodles… but one poodle doodle.

Fifi aspires to model someday...

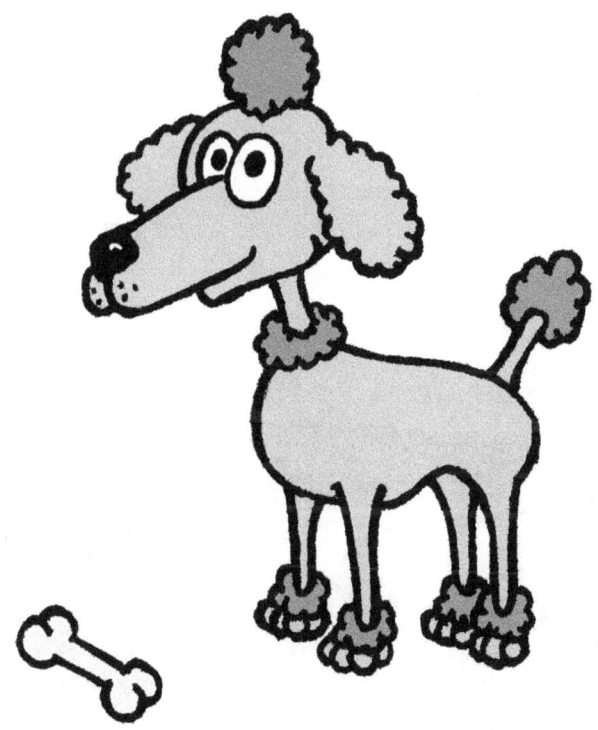

...for balloon animals.

Matt the marmot

August					
					#40
				22	

Meet Matt von Pelt, the marmot.

Matt likes to lay very flat.

When Matt finds a rock that's flat,

He spreads himself thin on it.

And that is that.

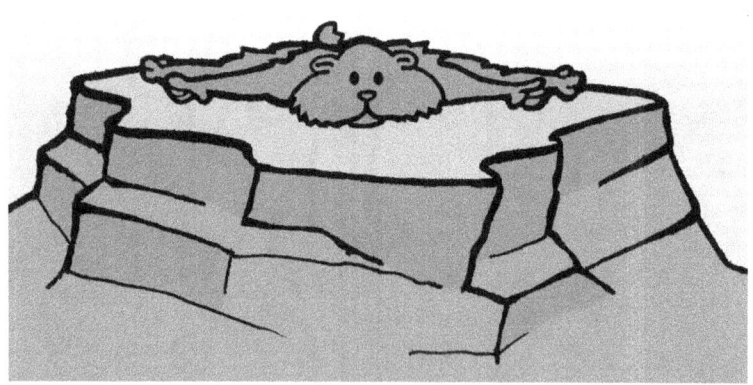

This doodle was inspired by a photo from my friend, Tracy.

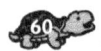

While hiking an undisclosed trail in the San Juan Mountains, summer 2009…

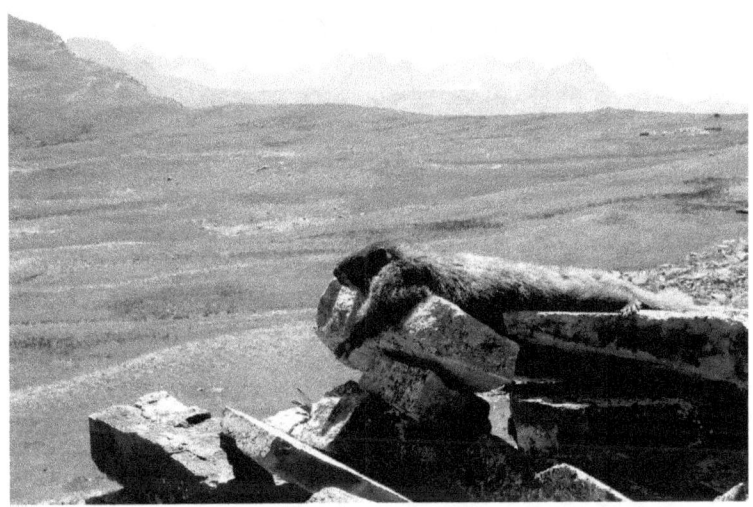

I didn't even notice the marmot until I was nearly upon him. Then, I thought he was dead because he was so flat and still! He looked like a fur pelt. After I got the picture, he turned his head and bared his teeth at me. I got the message and backed away slowly!

~ *Tracy*

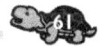

Beetle mania

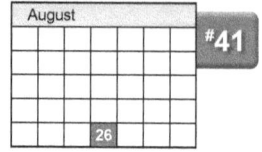

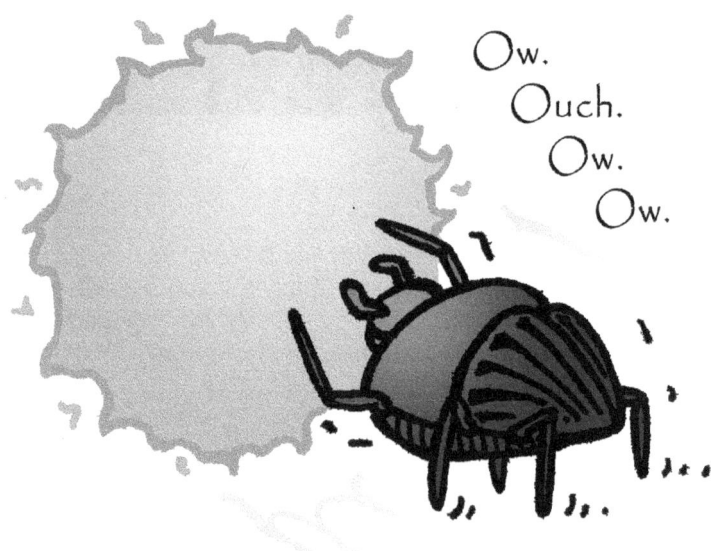

Almost three thousand years ago the ancient Egyptians believed that the sun was pushed across the sky by a giant scarab beetle.

They drew heiroglyphs on papyrus paper, carved them into stone, and made neat amulets and other jewelry depicting the scarab.

Can you imagine that beetle's job? Pushing, shoving, pushing, shoving, heaving and rolling that giant ball of fire across the sky with only six legs? Don't get me started on the smell of sunburned beetle. Get that guy some sunblock!

Ow.
Ouch.
Ow.
Ow.

August					#42
31				

Not so slow anymore

A request last week to draw a turtle driving a Camaro raised a few questions in my mind regarding what kind of car a turtle would actually choose. Muscle or mileage? Domestic or import? Hard top or convertible?

And what would his license plate say?

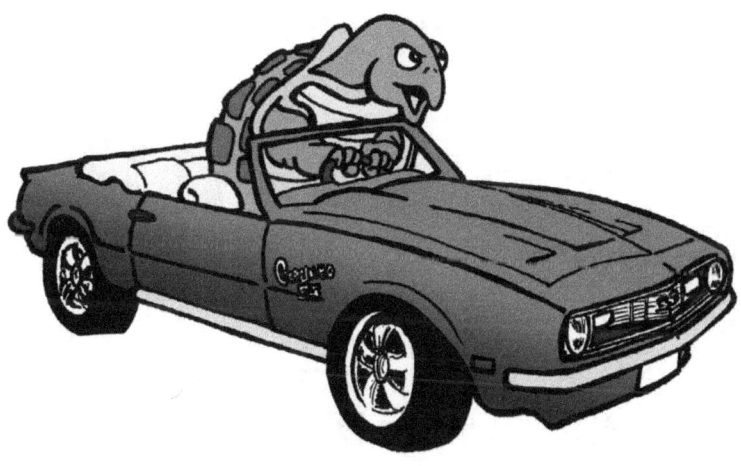

[Thanks, JK, for the suggestion!]

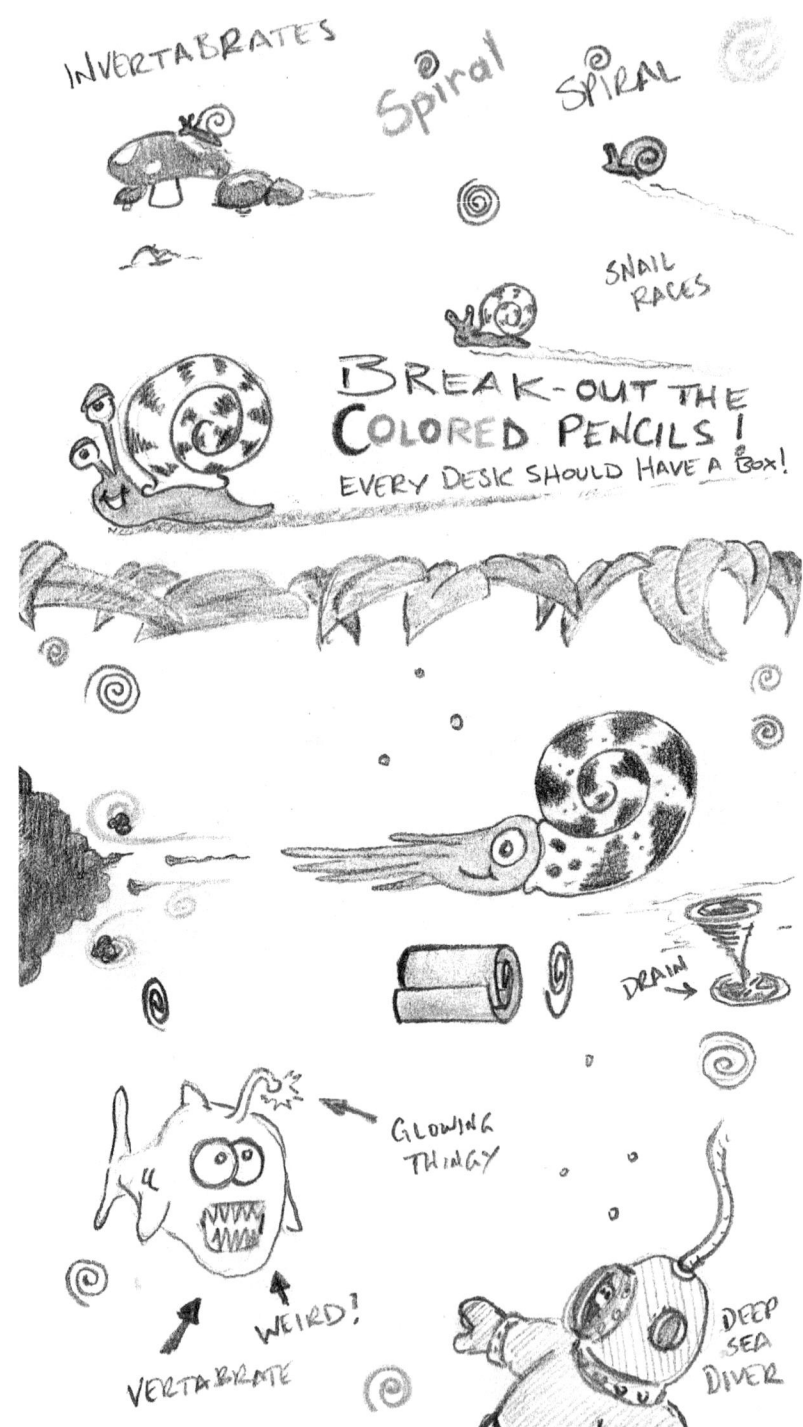

September

The days are cooling off and I'm bouncing back and forth again between pen and pencil. We have seen some wonderful wildlife thus far this summer. Elk, deer, fox, coyote and even a black bear walking through a friend's back yard.

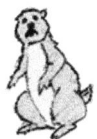

Don't try to weasel your way out of this one

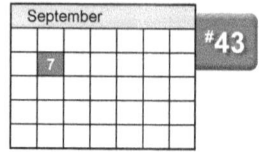

Our woodland friends, the weasels, have a bad reputation for being sneaky thieves. They're painted as untrustworthy skulkers, always up to no good.

Well, I think they are playful, friendly, likable creatures, who are neither sneaky nor thieves.

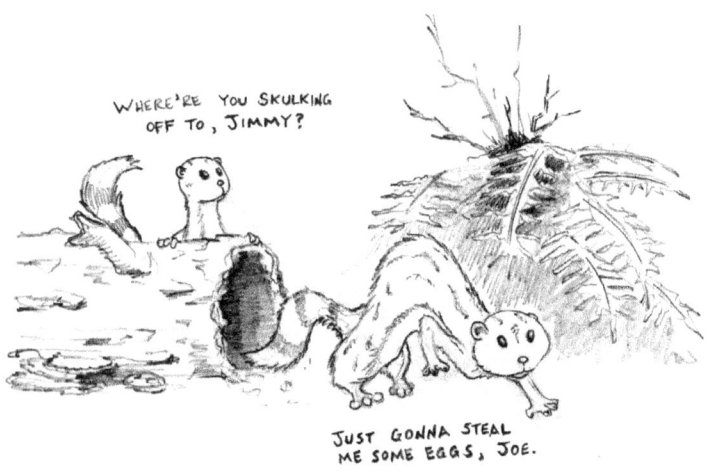

WHERE'RE YOU SKULKING OFF TO, JIMMY?

JUST GONNA STEAL ME SOME EGGS, JOE.

I stand corrected.

September						#44
14						

Little gray-headed birds

We went camping this weekend in Meuller State Park (Colorado) and enjoyed the cool air and high country with good friends. It rained Friday night and then a cold front blew through Saturday, deluging us Saturday night with a chilling rain.

Sunday morning the sun came out and with it the camp-site was full of energetic little bluegray-headed birds that hopped around, pecking at goodies among the pine needles. They were dark-eyed juncos, and it was beautiful to see their little colored heads bobbing around the forest floor.

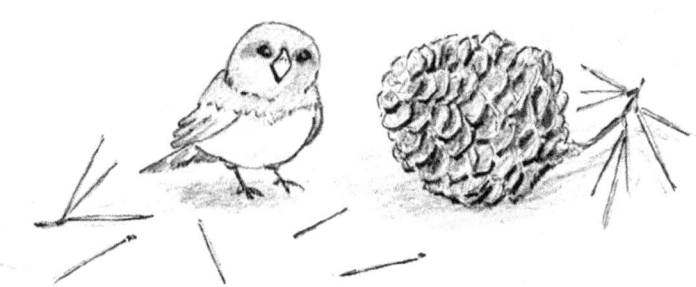

The conversation

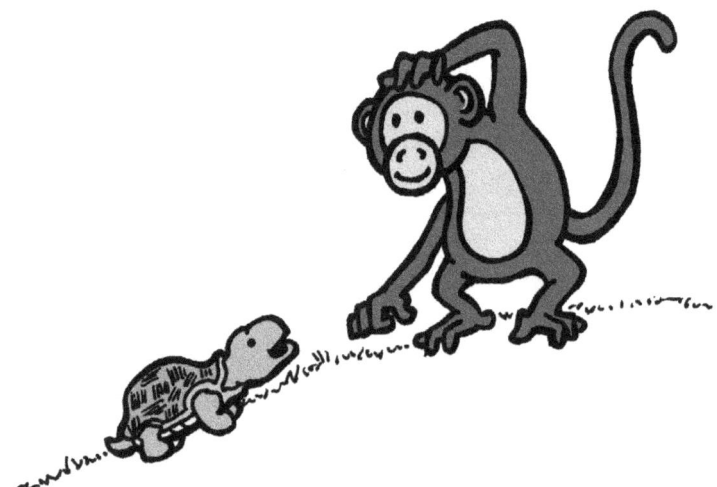

I'm leaving what they're talking about up to your imagination.

Sleep tight!

Bed bugs nibble on us when we're sleeping to drink tiny bits of our blood. We wouldn't notice them if it weren't for the fact that their bites make us itch. Since they normally do their business in the dark, we almost never see them.

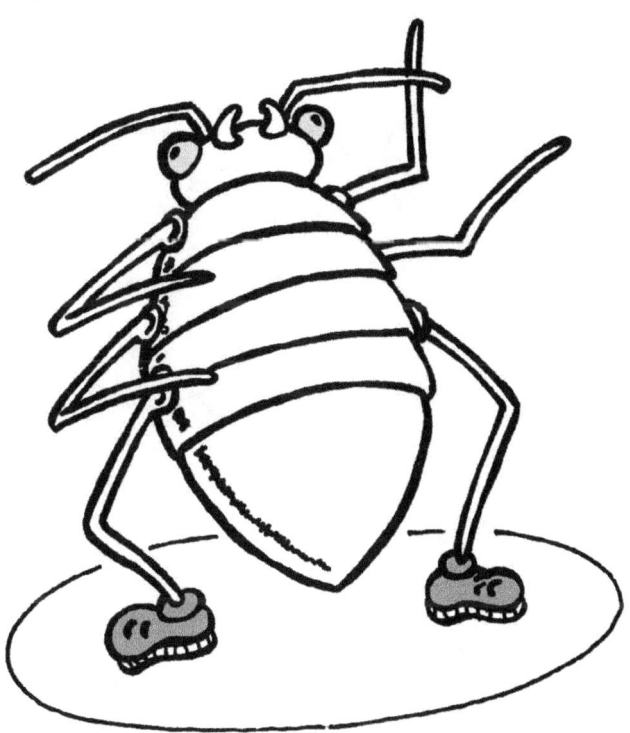

I WEAR MY SHOES TO BED FOR A QUICK GET-AWAY WHEN THE LIGHTS COME ON.

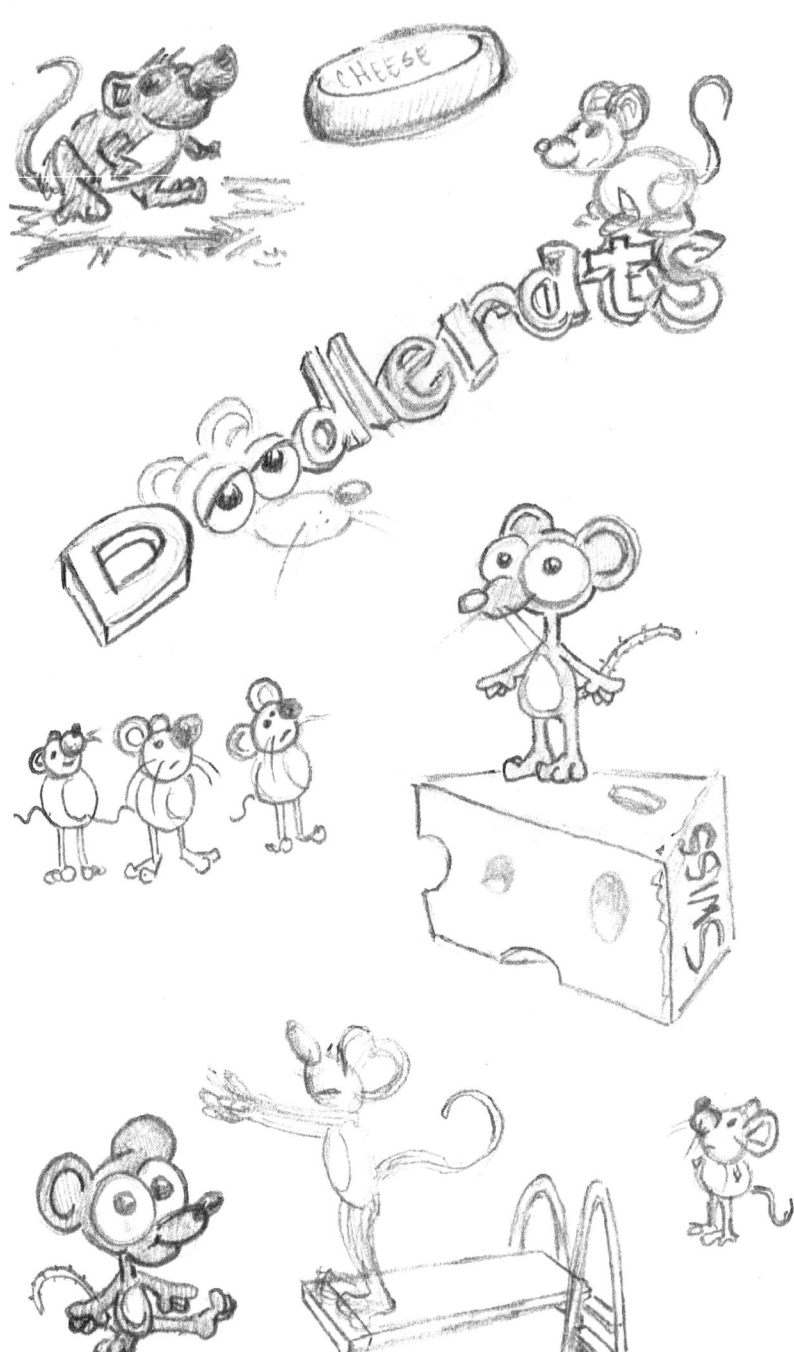

October

Something about Autumn makes me introspective.
Maybe it has something to do with how the leaves
start changing, the year begins winding down and
the correlation we make between the seasons and our
own mortality.

This year has been fantastic for reconnecting with old
friends and long-ago acquaintances. Voices from the
past have surfaced, not to haunt me, but to remind
me of what a full and rich life I'm living.

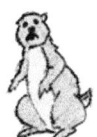

And the winner is...

I decided recently to give up eating meat. It is for a variety of reasons and I'm not going to get all crazy about it. It's kind of like a test of will power. Lots more veggies, fruit and grain in my diet.

I'm not going cold-turkey (ha!) on all meats just yet, but decided to start with beef. I'm not sure if I'll ever phase out fish and I haven't decided whether chicken or pork will be next on the list.

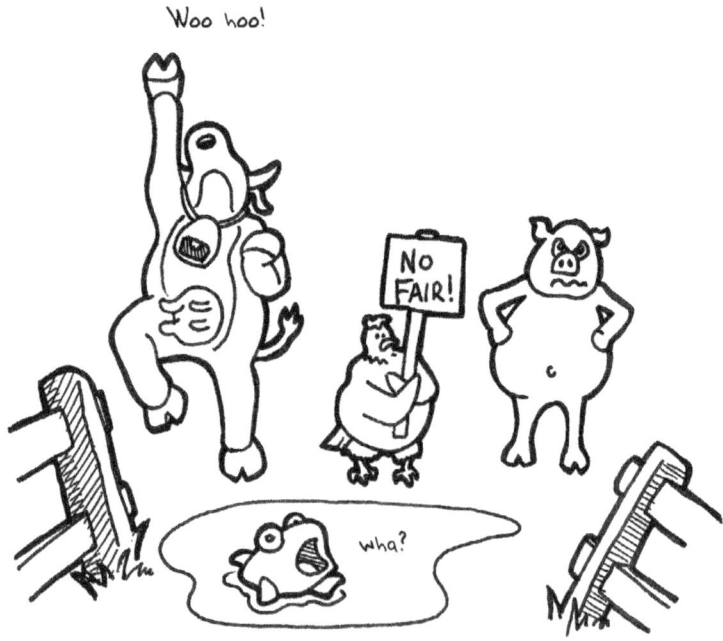

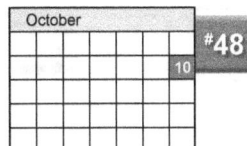

Pachyderm Picasso

What's this one called?

Squashed art critic.

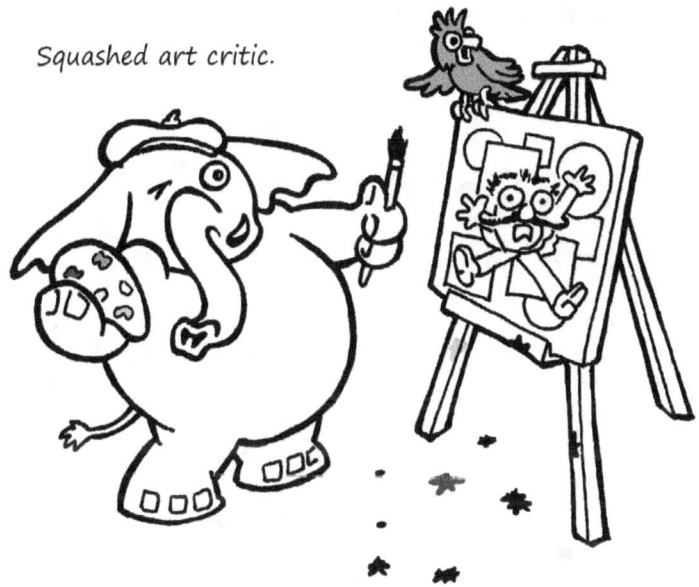

(Sigh) If only we could…

Just passing through

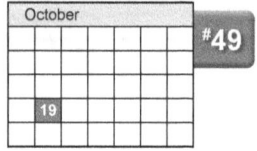

I like to draw bears, though they always tend to look like stuffed teddy bears rather than real ones.

To make these slightly truer to nature, I included their claws. It doesn't really stop them from being cute and cuddly. Just makes them a little more dangerous.

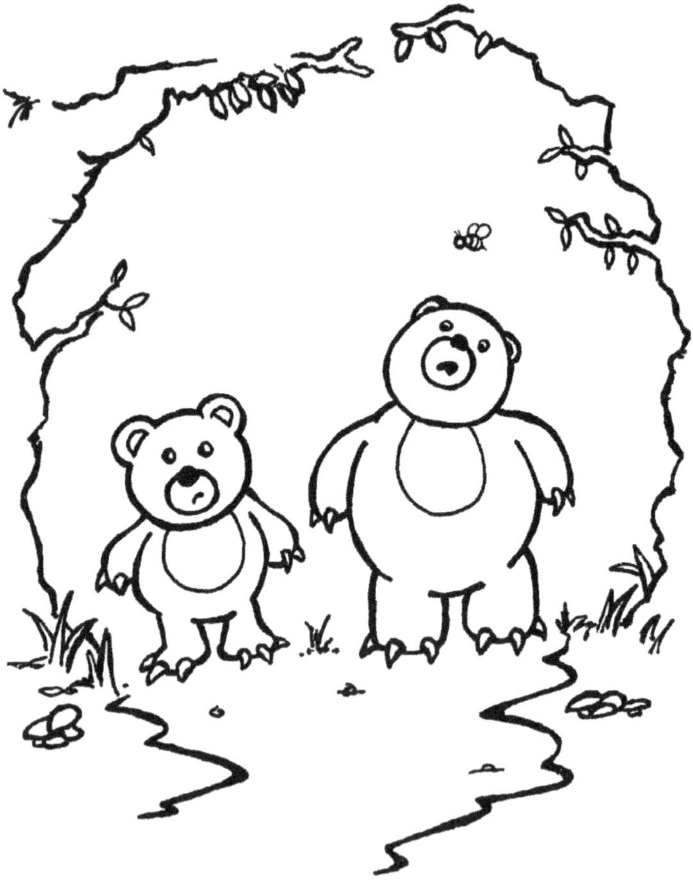

Thom Phelps

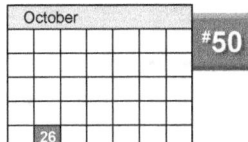

#50

Snaring trick-or-treaters

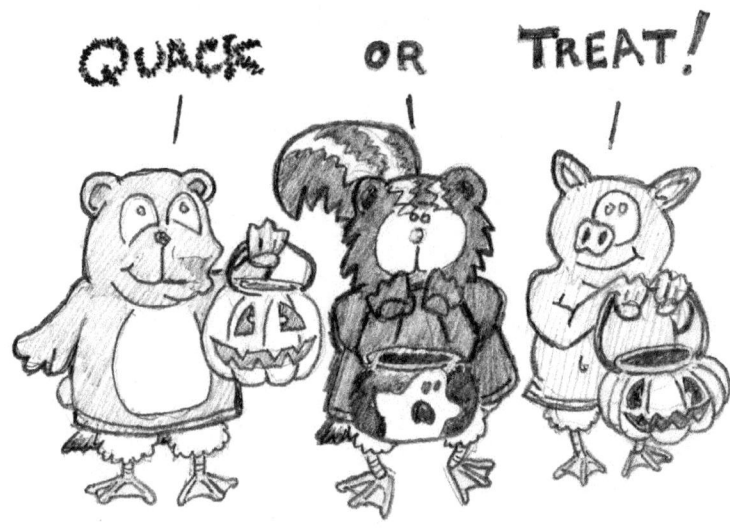

While trick-or-treating with his American cousins in Michigan, Jacques' Canadian accent gives him away again.

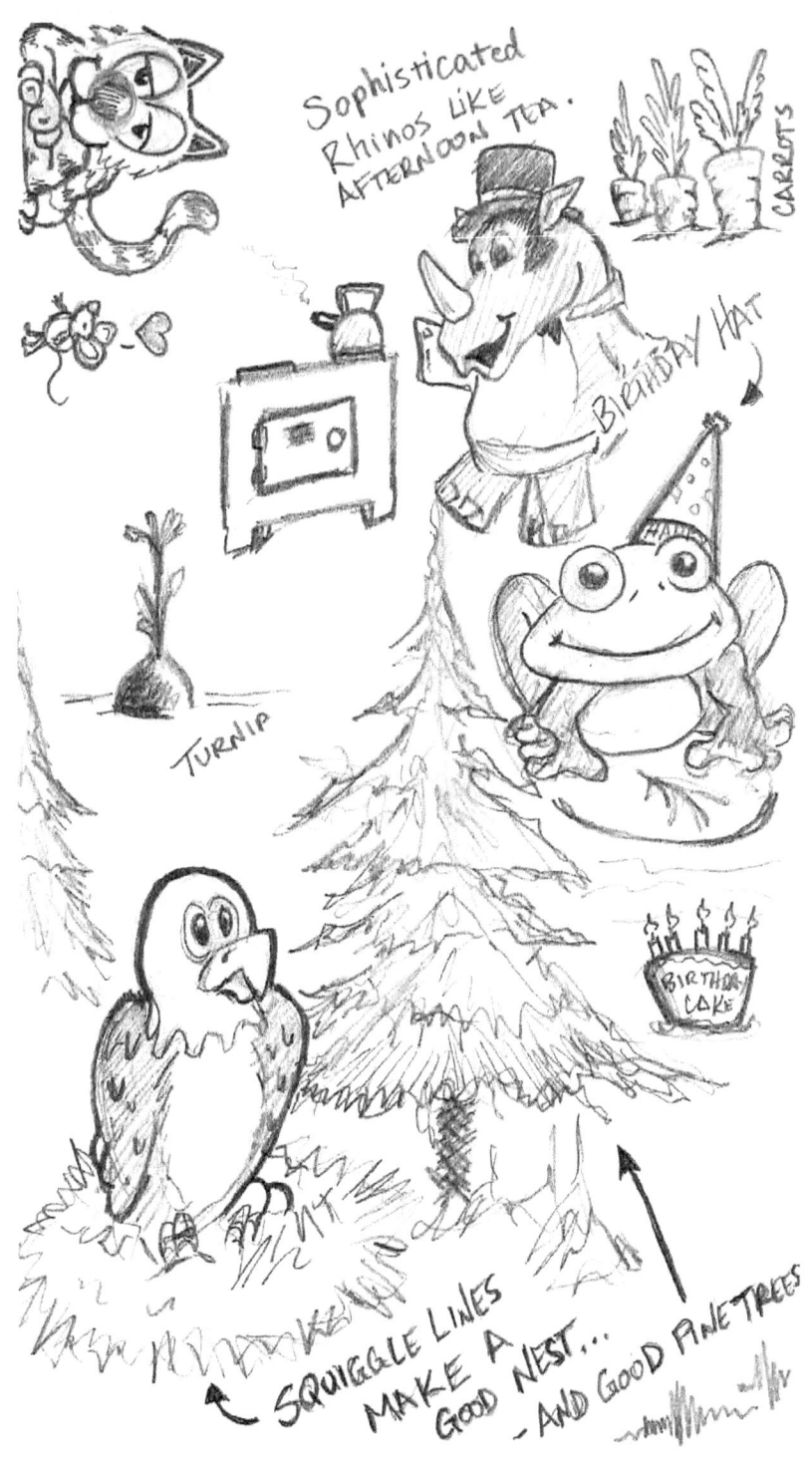

Sophisticated Rhinos Like AFTERNOON TEA.

CARROTS

BIRTHDAY HAT

TURNIP

BIRTHDAY CAKE

SQUIGGLE LINES MAKE A GOOD NEST... — AND GOOD PINE TREES

November

I'm finding myself humming Christmas songs I picked up from walking through the grocery store or waiting in line somewhere. Seemed like only yesterday I was getting my camping gear ready and before I knew it, I've put it all away, had fun at a Halloween party, and am prepping to decorate my house with strands of lights.

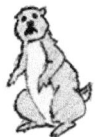

So long, shrimp!

November					
	3				#51

Pack your bags, prawn.

Catch a cab, crab.

Hasta la vista, lobster.

I dropped "shellfish" last week from the menu. I'm not sure why this guy is angry, though. He should be happy to be off the chopping block (or out of the fishing net). Maybe I just drew his mouth upside-down...

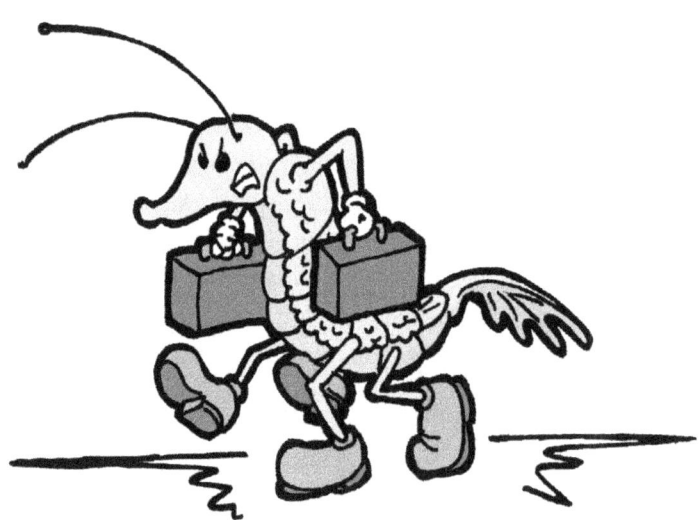

November						
			5			

Eight weeks to go

Though I live where it's almost always sunny, the grass has faded to a yellow-brown crispiness and the trees have dropped their leaves in preparation for a chilly winter's sleep. Only eight weeks of snaring woodland creatures left for 2009. My, how time flies. It's been fun so far and looks like it will continue to be a positive creative outlet for me.

I'm not entirely sure porcupines hibernate.

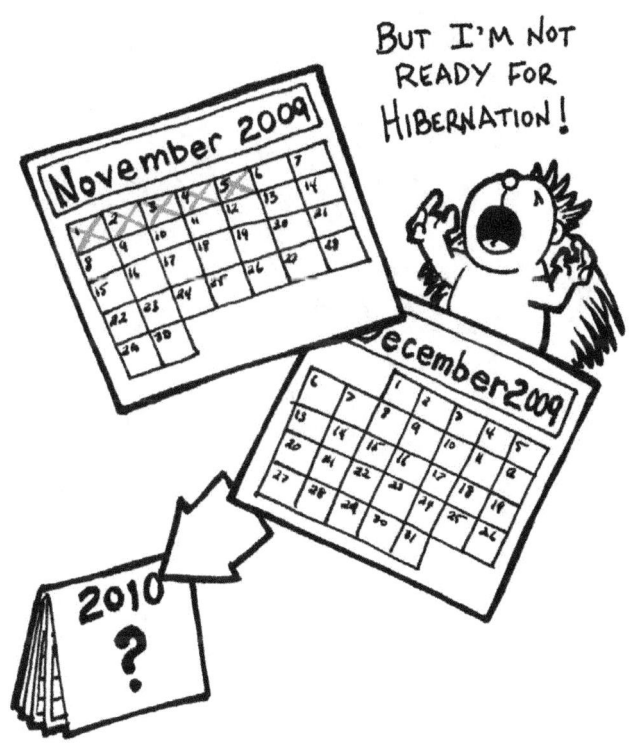

You know what it's like

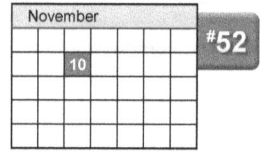

Mother Nature says, "it's bed time," but a certain someone refuses to hit the hay.

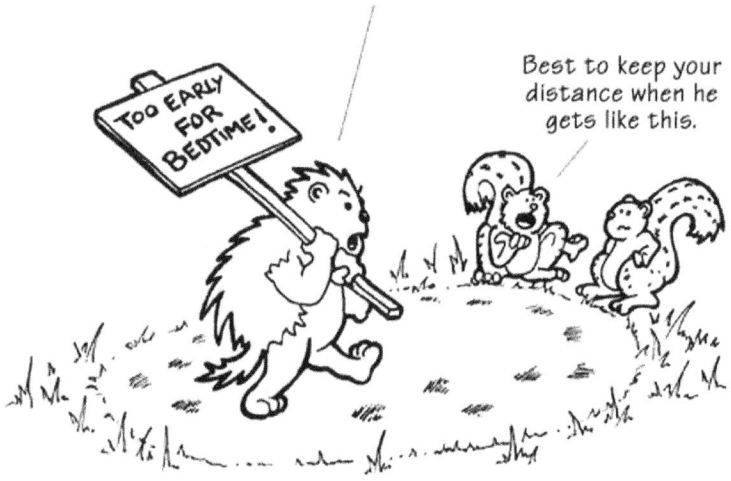

There are lots of reasons we need more seasons!
There are lots of reasons we need more seasons!

#52! I reached my goal a little ahead of schedule. But there are more weeks left to go!

November

17

#53

Tenacious D

Of the martial arts woodland creatures, the most fearsome is the badger. Ferocious, tenacious, unstoppable, and sly, he is an unbeatable foe.

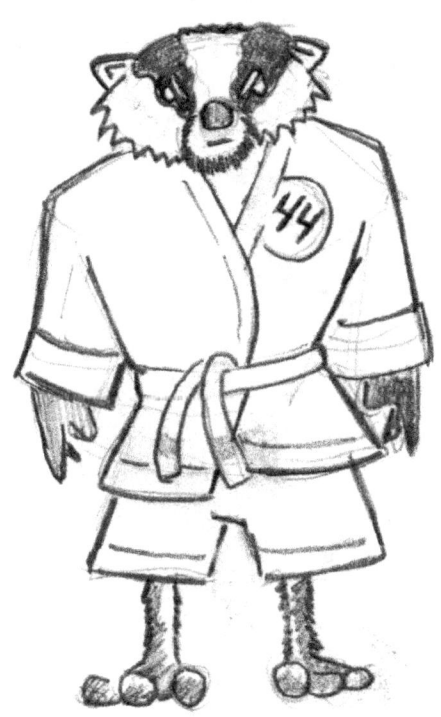

His favorite form? The Crazy Leg move, of course.

"Look at my leg! It's way up there, getting all CRAZY. What's it going to do? I don't know, because it has a mind of its own. Come closer and look. Look at the crazy leg!"

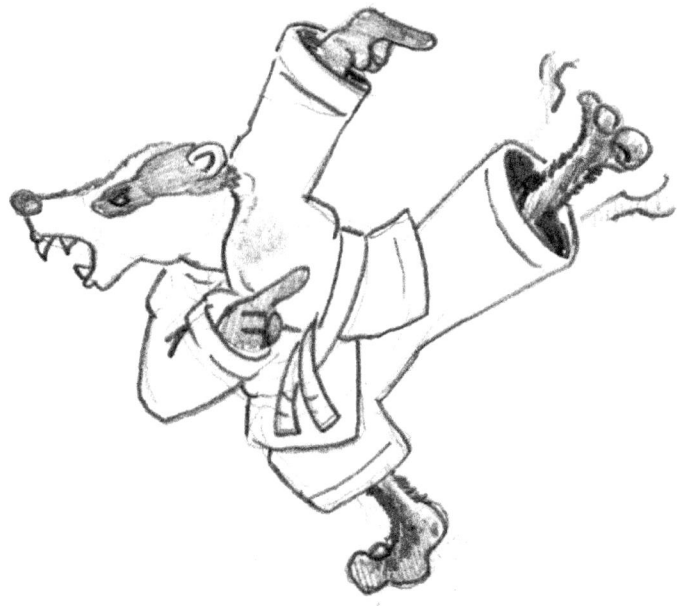

There is no defense.

November #54

23

It's what they do

What else would you expect from box turtles?

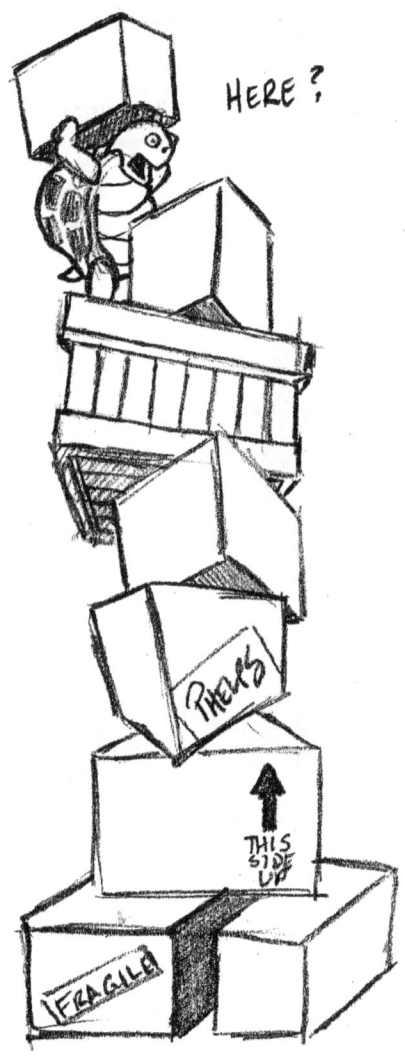
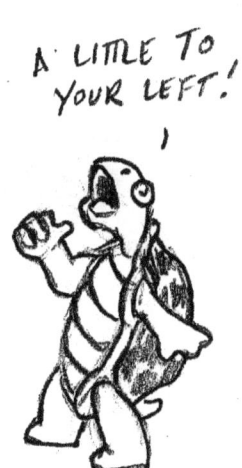

Condos for scorpions

A gorgeous Thanksgiving weekend in Austin, Texas.

We enjoyed a little yard work of moving some old cinder blocks. Yes, there were scorpions and centipedes. It's Texas, after all.

To scorpions, a pile of cinder blocks must be like fancy high-rise condominiums. Nice view!

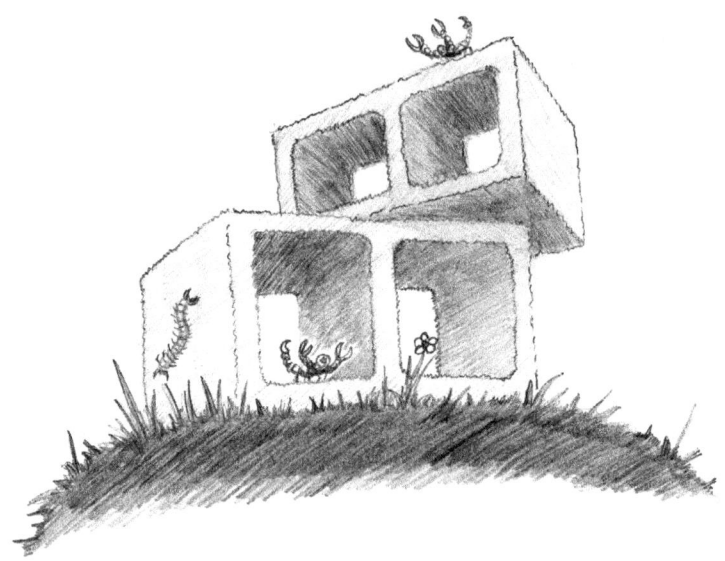

December

My doodle quest for 2009 is almost over and I'm sad for it, not knowing what 2010 has in store for my pen and pencil. Hopefully just more of the same. Still, it's been fun to have the goal of drawing something every weeek and getting to share it with friends.

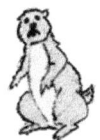

Cute rodents

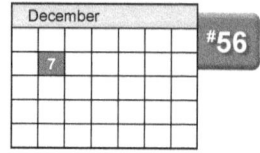

Even rats are cute when they're young.

Not to offend any rat-lovers out there. Each has its own personality and temperament, I'm sure. And beauty is only fur deep. But I've always found rats less appealing than say hamsters, gerbils, or guinea pigs.

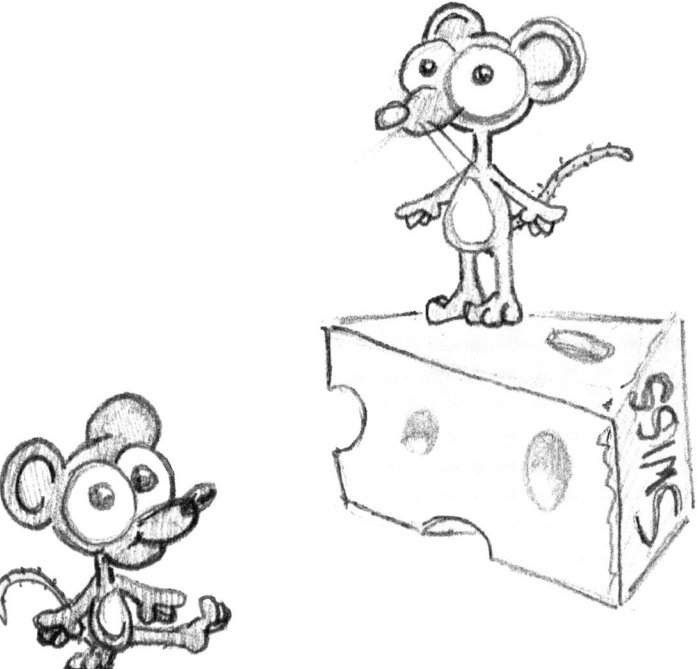

Thom Phelps

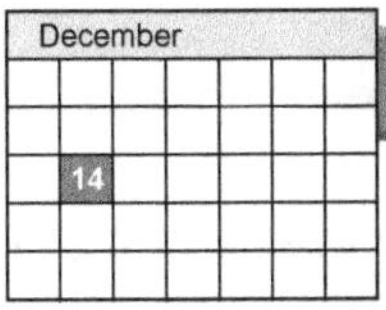

December

14

#57

Neither jelly nor a fish

And you definitely would not want to spread it on toast.

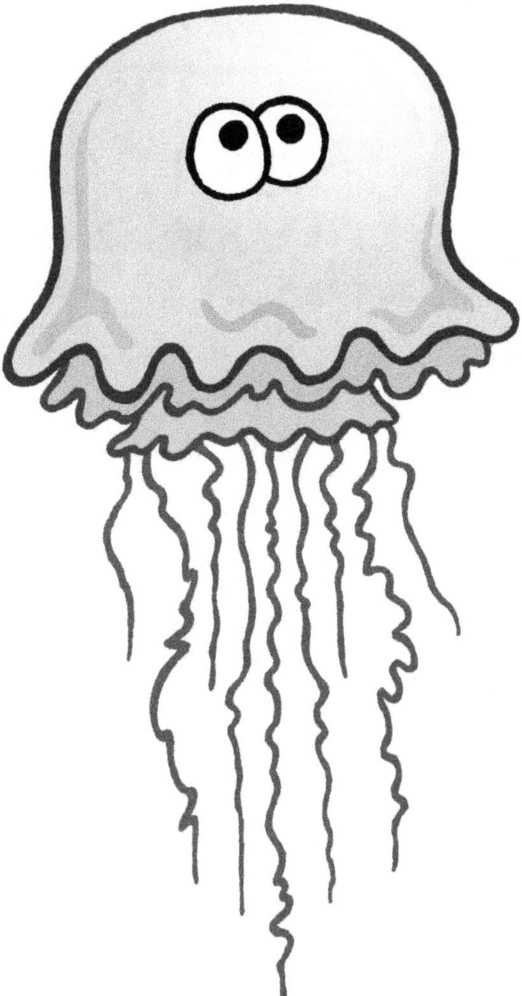

I'm more of a jam person myself. Strawberry preserves being my favorite.

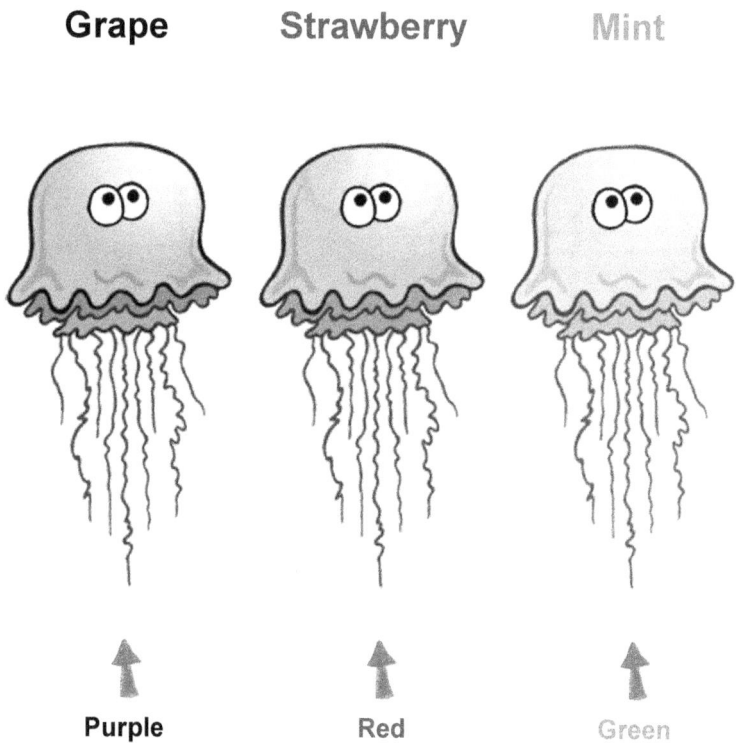

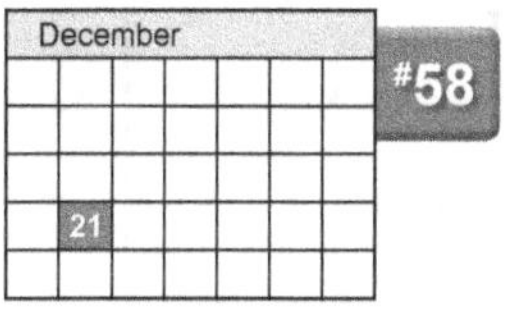

December					
					#58
21					

That's no llama

She's an alpaca, and her name is Mahogany's Lunessa.

I made a pencil holder for a friend's desk, as an office Christmas present, that's based off of this doodle. He raises alpacas and Lunessa is part of his herd. Her photo is on the web and I drew from that.

I like her goofy expression. I wonder what she's thinking?

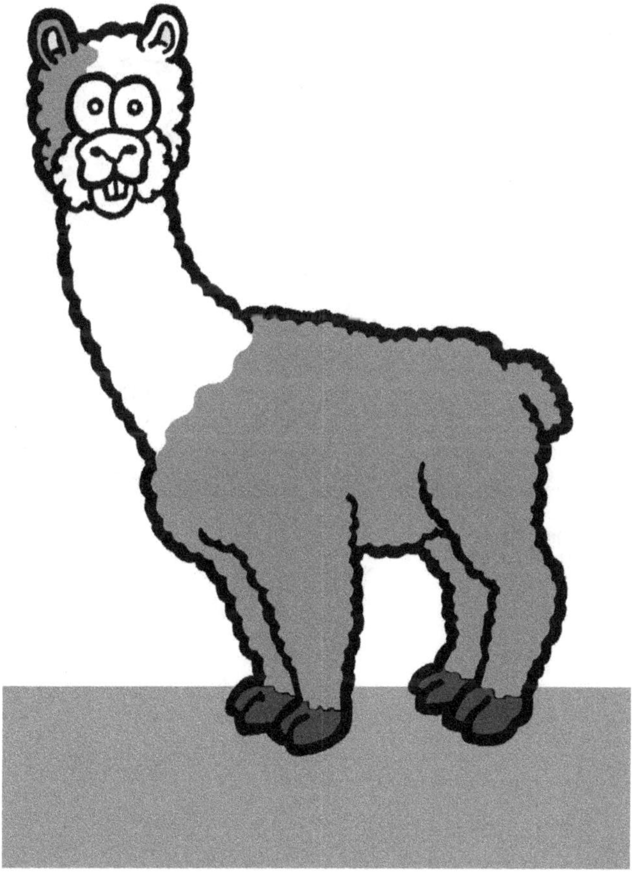

The days are getting longer

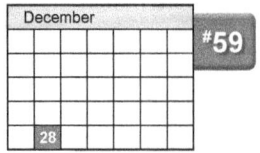

The shortest day of the year came and went last week in the blink of an eye, or so it seemed. Now, though winter just started, with the days getting longer it's going to start feeling like spring is just around the corner.

Yay!

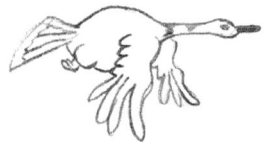

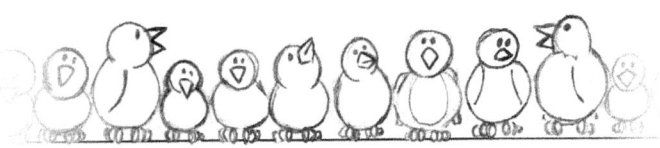

I think migration every year is too expensive.

Cheep.

This is the last doodle posting for 2009.

The following pages include two full-page doodles that I drew during the year. Including a "how to draw a cat" lesson that I did during a layover in DIA airport.

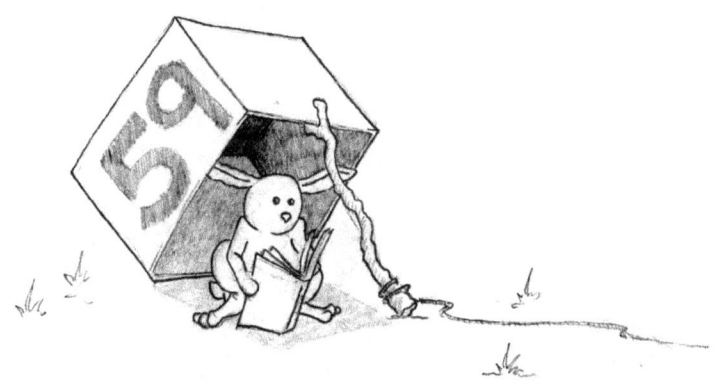

This is the first doodle for 2010.

"A hare-raising novel."

Easy as A·B·C.

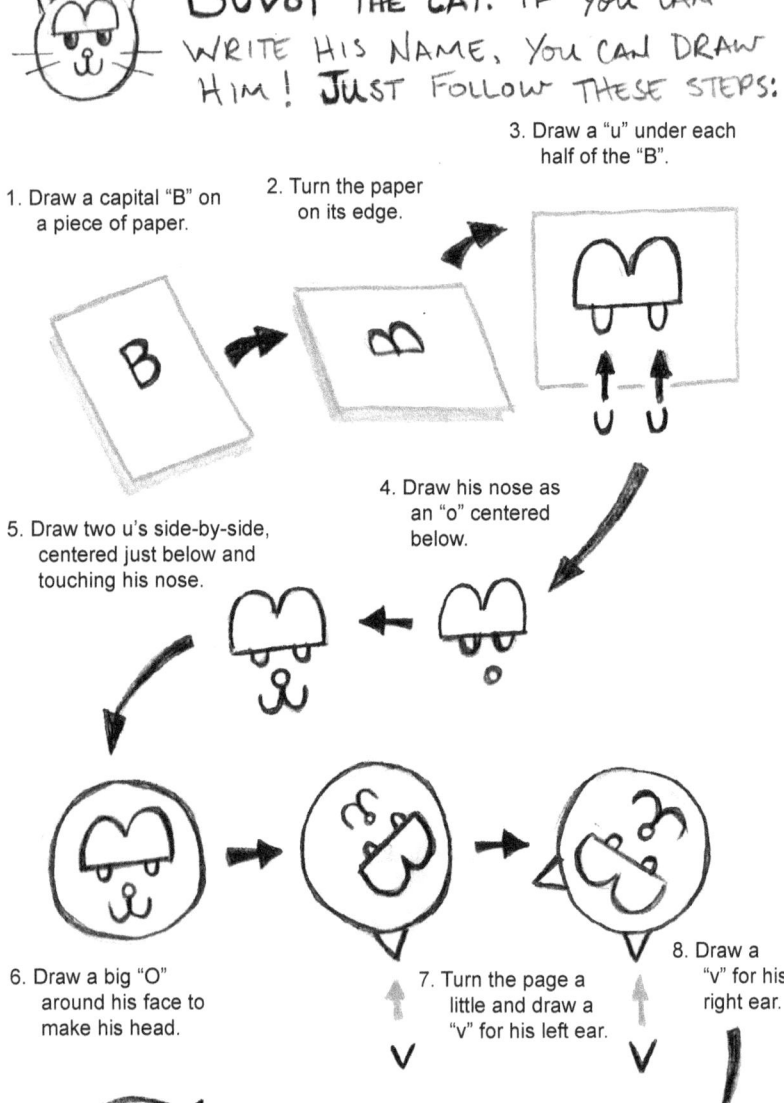

Buvol THE CAT. IF YOU CAN WRITE HIS NAME, YOU CAN DRAW HIM! JUST FOLLOW THESE STEPS:

1. Draw a capital "B" on a piece of paper.

2. Turn the paper on its edge.

3. Draw a "u" under each half of the "B".

4. Draw his nose as an "o" centered below.

5. Draw two u's side-by-side, centered just below and touching his nose.

6. Draw a big "O" around his face to make his head.

7. Turn the page a little and draw a "v" for his left ear.

8. Draw a "v" for his right ear.

9. Fill in his eyes a little with color.

10. Turn the page and draw an "I" for each of his whiskers.

Ta-da! You're done.

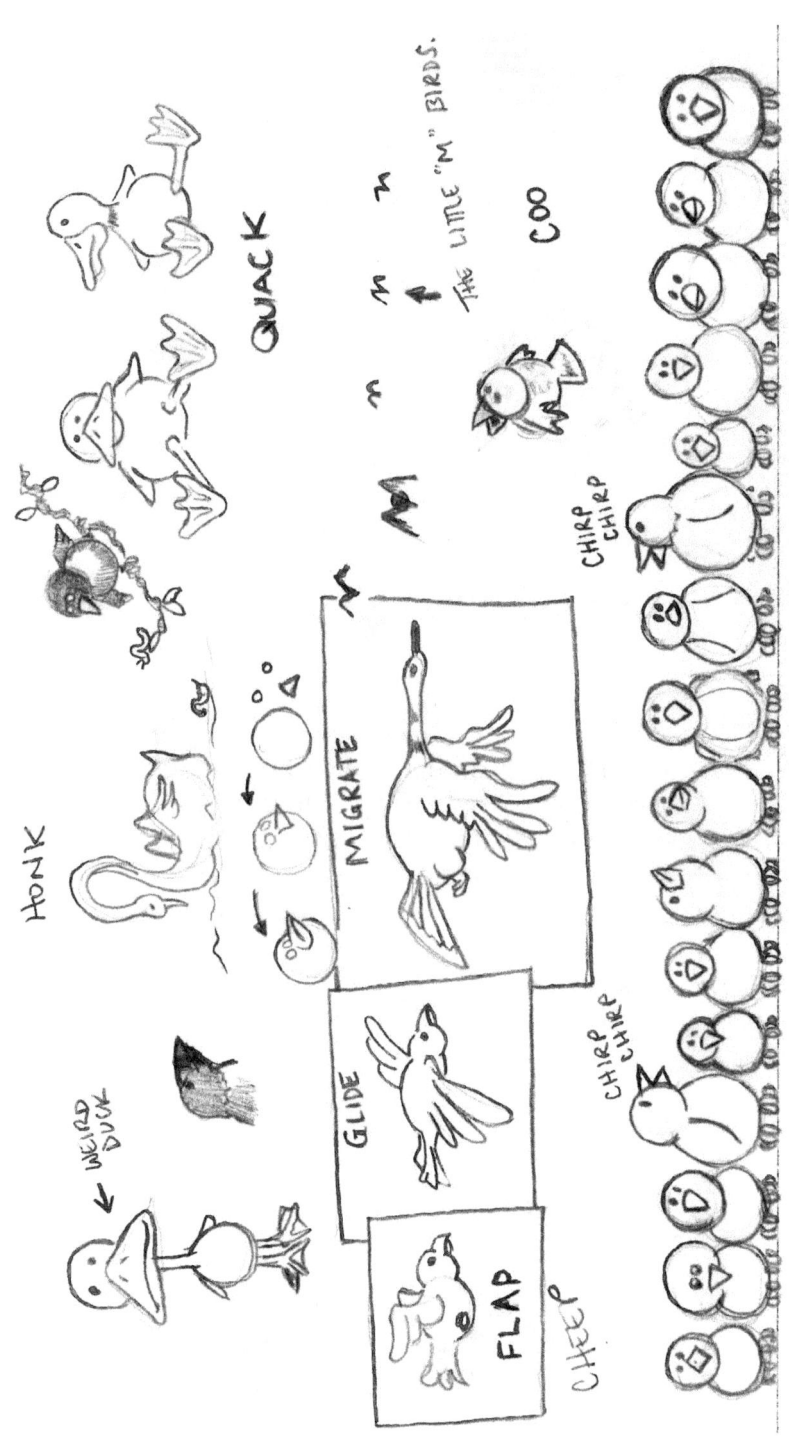

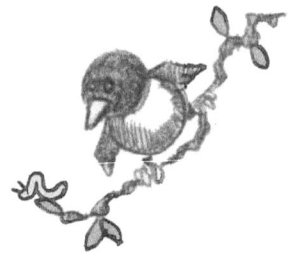

About the author

Thom Phelps grew up in Texas but loved the Colorado mountains so much that in 1997 he and his wife moved to Colorado Springs. They have lived there, happily, ever since.

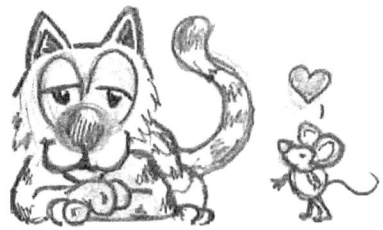

www.ingramcontent.com/pod-product-compliance
Lightning Source LLC
Chambersburg PA
CBHW071235170526
45165CB00003B/1100